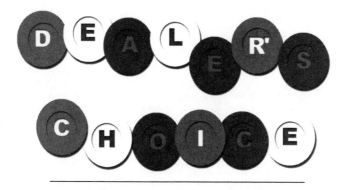

THE COMPLETE HANDBOOK OF
SATURDAY NIGHT POKER

JAMES ERNEST, PHIL FOGLIO & MIKE SELINKER

OVERLOOK DUCKWORTH

New York • Woodstock • London

First published in 2005 by
Overlook Duckworth, Peter Mayer Publishers, Inc.
New York, Woodstock, and London

NEW YORK:
141 Wooster Street
New York, NY 10012

WOODSTOCK:
One Overlook Drive
Woodstock, NY 12498
www.overlookpress.com
[for individual orders, bulk and special sales, contact our Woodstock office]

LONDON:
Gerald Duckworth & Co. Ltd.
90-93 Cowcross Street
London EC1M 6BF
inquiries@duckworth-publishers.co.uk
www.ducknet.co.uk

Cataloging-in-Publication Data is available from the Library of Congress
and the British Library

Book design and type formatting by Bernard Schleifer
Manufactured in the United States of America
FIRST EDITION
ISBN 1-58567-654-3
ISBN 0-7156-3357-0 (UK)
1 3 5 7 9 8 6 4 2

CONTENTS

INTRODUCTION

Since the dawn of history, man has struggled to take money away from other man at a friendly game of cards. Okay, perhaps not since the dawn of History. Perhaps since the invention of money. And games. And cards.

The point is that somewhere along the way they started making up crazy poker games and playing them in a structure we know as "Dealer's Choice." It's an evening of poker where the deal passes around the table, and every dealer on his turn may choose, perhaps from a list, perhaps from his own head, a new and crazy way to play.

We think this came about because of a slow devaluation of the currency of poker. As nickels, dimes, and quarters (enough to get you a meal at the beginning of the century) became more and more valueless, casual poker players had two choices: raise the stakes and play for foldin' money, or make up wacky rules that get more money into play. It probably didn't happen overnight. Someone calls a wild card, someone else lets people draw twice, and so on. Pretty soon, though, you have a runaway train on your hands, as shown by the explosion of different games in this book.

Dealer's choice poker is a wild animal, and we've done our

best to tame it. This book contains hints on how to set up your own house game, how to describe your own house rules, and how to think strategically about the game. You'll also find a list of more than two hundred poker games; we wrote about the classics, and then, being game designers as we are, we made up the rest. Most of the games are good, and most of them have been played at least once. You can play them all yourself and make your own decisions. By our best guess, that will give you about twelve hours of fun. If you like some of them enough to play more than once, the fun will continue.

Chapter 1

HOSTING YOUR
POKER GAME

Okay, it's Friday afternoon, and tomorrow night you're going to host your first Saturday night poker game. What do you need?

You need this book. Actually, you need, let's say, eight copies. One for each of your guests. Maybe one more for your glove compartment. You never know when a poker game will break out in the front seat of your car. The more books you buy, the more royalties we earn, which means lavish trips to Las Vegas to learn more critical information we can share with you. But more importantly, you'll have the confidence that comes with having too much stuff.

You need some other things too. These are less important than multiple copies of this book, but they are important nonetheless. You certainly don't want to be standing at the register at McDonald's at 6:30 Saturday night wondering where you might get your hands on enough nickels, dimes, and quarters to play poker. Assuming you have even figured out how many nickels, dimes, and quarters you need.

This chapter poses the tough questions you should be asking yourself while arranging your game, and then answers them cleverly and concisely. First up: humans.

WHO'S COMING?

You obviously need players at your poker game. They don't have to know how to play poker (this is frankly a strike against them), but they should be smart, easygoing, and willing to learn new things. Start by inviting everybody you like. If four to eight people say "yes," you have your guest list. If not, start calling the people you like a little less.

Let your players know what kind of game to expect. Some people claim to love "real poker," so they'll pitch a fit when you call some of the mutant games listed in Chapter Three. If all eight players are in the mood for a whole night of Texas Hold 'Em, that's great. But if seven people want that, and one player wants to make up new games all night long, be prepared for friction.

Poker, especially the dealer's choice variety, needs at least four players to be interesting. Most games in this book function well in the six- to eight-player range, but (with the notable exception of Hold 'Em) break down quickly in higher numbers. The optimal number of people to invite is probably seven to ten. Someone's going to be late, and someone's going to leave early, so you'll be happy if there are always six to eight people at the table.

In a dealer's choice game, players should be interested in trying new games and able to think on their feet. There are more than two hundred games in this book, and you'll certainly be adding more as you play. Most require pretty quick analysis of which hands are good and bad. This book only gives the barest nod to improving your strategy on these mindbenders, so you're pretty much on your own. If your friends feel they need the crutch of pre-baked strategy, they should stick to books by people named Sklansky and games that end with "Seven Card Stud."

WHAT STAKES SHOULD I PLAY?

You should play at the financial level at which everyone in the game can feel comfortable. No one is going to get rich at this game, so no one should walk away feeling like they got poor.

You may have a few players who refuse to play if the stakes are too *low*. Like we said, no one's going to get rich at a nickel game, even if you are playing for quarters. Try to seduce these sophisticates with the "we're here to have fun" argument, and if that doesn't work, figure out how to get by without them.

Inviting players from your own tax bracket is far from the dumbest thing on Earth. If you invite a guy who lights cigars with $100 bills, you may have to convince him to pretend that the money matters as much as it does to, say, the normal humans in the room. Players with big bankrolls and no respect for money can have a terrible effect on the game, calling and raising when they should be folding, and not blinking when they have to match a $30 pot. It's not that they won't lose money in the long run; they will. But in the meantime they can put the game through intolerable swings, and that may drive other players out for good.

To tell the truth, at the level of nickels and dimes, it's actually hard to convince *anyone* that the game is for real money. That's why pot-doubling games were invented. But the rich guy is going to keep thinking it doesn't matter, even when the pot is up to $50. That's just no fun for anyone.

Ironically, the world's best players have a knack for forgetting that those plastic chips are worth thousands and thousands of dollars. So playing for nickels is good practice for the high-limit world. The difference is that these guys learned to play perfectly while the money still mattered to them, and now they can keep that edge while becoming detached from the money; on the other hand, you might be just learning bad habits because you don't care.

The dollar values in this book are all based on playing in a nickel-quarter game. That is, a nickel ante, with bets and raises ranging from 5 to 25 cents. If you play at another limit, it's easy to multiply the numbers in this book by whatever makes them right. For example, if you're playing Baseball in a $40-$200 game, you might decide that receiving a 4 lets you buy another card for $80. (And, if you're playing Baseball for $40-$200, you can check yourself into a psychiatric ward tomorrow morning. Go ahead, you can afford it.)

Depending on the number of pot-matching games you play, a nickel-quarter game can cost an unlucky player anywhere from $5 to $20 a night, a little more if he plays crazy. If this doesn't seem like enough money to your group, double the bets to 10 and 50 cents, or just raise the maximum bet to 50 cents, while keeping the ante at a nickel. If you're playing 5-50, most numbers and prices in this book are still fine.

WHEN SHOULD I PLAY?

Seven A.M. is not a great time for a poker game—unless you're just wrapping up. Then it's a *great* time for a poker game.

A typical poker game will break up after about four hours, give or take three. Four hours is enough time for about 120 hands of the same simple game (Texas Hold 'Em, Seven Card Stud), or about 40 hands of dealer's choice games. The wacky games take longer to learn and longer to play. That is, the gap between "What're we playin', Zeke?" and "And the first card is . . ." can be as long as the game itself, and some of the best games take multiple rounds to finish. Help Zeke decide what to play by encouraging him to flip to a random page in Chapter Three before he has to deal, or by just suggesting he call Seven Card Stud if he can't think of anything better.

Your playing time should be structured around when people get off work, and when they have to be back at work. We like Friday and Saturday nights, though Sunday afternoons aren't bad either if your deity allows it. The expected moment at which your neighbors are prone to scream "Keep it down, or we're callin' the cops!" is another possible limiting factor. When you can manage it, play at someone's mansion by a lake, where you can make as much noise as you like, and even kill unruly folks, if it comes to that.

If the game starts at 6 P.M., you will have to feed everyone. If it starts at 9:00, people will feed themselves beforehand. 7:30 is just confusing enough to go either way. Your opinion of whether feeding people is a good thing or a bad thing must come from within, but remember this: food and cards don't mix. More about this subject below.

In our neck of the woods, midnight is a critical time. This is when we feel we have permission to start playing wildly, calling bloody games, and parting the fools we call friends from their money in the most efficient manner possible. The clock strikes twelve, the big stacks consolidate quickly, checks are written, farewells are said, and cars begin fleeing the driveway. It's an efficient way to break up any party.

If you don't want to drive people home in tears, there is another option: you can just tell them to leave. The best method is to call "one more round," which means that everyone, starting with you, gets to deal one more game. Since some people will call multi-hand games with their last option, you're still in for a good 45 minutes when you say this. If that's still too long, set a timer and make people leave when it beeps.

IS POKER LEGAL HERE?

Good question. If you have the choice of what state to play in, we recommend Alaska. Maybe. Or on a cruise ship. *Definitely* on a cruise ship.

However, since you probably can't move your game, you're going to have to play in whatever sad state you live in. We're not lawyers, but if we were, we'd probably say something like, "We couldn't possibly advise you of the legality of a house poker game in your locale due to liability issues." In other words, your carefree fun isn't worth even a tiny fraction of our ass.

If you're concerned, and maybe you should be, you can ask your state gambling commission whether home poker games are allowed. Be especially aware of the rules if you're going to invite your friend Ralph, the undercover vice cop. (Actually, if you're friends with Ralph, just ask him.)

Don't rely on what you've heard second-hand, because it's almost certainly wrong. Some jurisdictions allow home games under certain very weird restrictions, some are a lot more lenient, some don't have rules at all. Here's the important thing: Most have better things to do than bust up your little poker game. There are something like 60 million poker players in the U.S. and nary a one of them goes to jail for playing cards for nickels. Without some better reason to bust you, the local cops are not likely to drag you, your friends, and a fifth of the nation's population to jail.

It's difficult to say where home poker is legal, because laws change all the time. There are many states where "social gam-bling" among adults—that is, gambling where the house is merely a player and takes no more than what a player would normally win—is explicitly legal. As of this writing those states seem to include Alaska, Arizona, Colorado, Connecticut, Hawaii, Kentucky, Maine, New Jersey, New York, Oregon, Texas, Washington, and Wyoming. Maybe more. But you didn't hear that from us, and it's probably wrong.

Oh yeah, one more thing: Whether poker is *legal* in your

state or not, it's *taxable* in all of them. So, you know, keep accurate records on acid-free paper.

WHAT SHOULD I PLAY ON?

Assuming you're still playing after all that warning, you will need a good table. Before you go out and buy a poker table be aware that you probably have a couple of choices around the house, and you may be able to improve what you have.

First, abandon the folding card table unless your game has only four players. Sure, it has a decent surface for shuffling and dealing, and it was only 20 bucks at Wal-Mart. But it's built for bridge, not for poker, and when you add even one more player, someone's going to have a table leg where his knees should be. A pair of these will seat six players comfortably and will be serviceable if you can tolerate the crack down the middle. Still, it's a little cramped.

Ideally, your table should have enough room for eight people, their chips, and their drinks, and its legs should be as unobtrusive as possible. A pedestal table is the best. Your table should be large enough to hold your group but small enough so everyone can reach into the middle (to grab their money). We suggest a round table with a diameter of 48 to 62 inches. We also suggest side tables for drinks and snacks, so there's more room on the main table for elbows.

You'll want a felt cover or tablecloth. If you are using a tablecloth, you can improve card- and chip-manipulation with a layer of eighth-inch thick open-cell foam underneath the cloth. If you can make a fitted felt cover, you'll be even happier.

For example, here are the three poker tables we own. The simplest one is at James's house. It's a 48" round pedestal table, good for up to seven players, with a 12" leaf that allows it to seat as many as nine.

Mike's table is a classic rectangular dining table 48" x 72" with all three leaves. He usually attracts loudmouthed spectators, so he likes the long edges. They do pose a problem, though, because it's hard to deal from the short ends. Casino poker tables are long because the dealer always sits in the middle. Mike sits at the end by the kitchen so he can be a gracious host, and has consequently gotten pretty good at flinging cards across the table. Not anywhere near the players they're supposed to go to, of course, but across the table nonetheless.

And then there's Phil's bona fide poker table, from a genuine Prohibition-era saloon. The 54" wooden roundtop rests on a pedestal of cast iron. When you remove the wooden lid, you find a leather playing surface surrounded by a well containing drink holders, brass trays for nickels (actually, these are ashtrays), and a friendly, old-timey antique smell. Phil inherited this from his great-grandfather, a New York saloonkeeper of the old school.

SHOULD I USE CHIPS OR COINS?

You can play with chips or coins, it's pretty much your choice. Chips are easier to count and play with, but they do cost money. Coins are cheaper to use, and the game can get started faster, since you skip the part where everyone has to buy chips.

Phil's game is a coin game. Players bring their boxes and bags of nickels and quarters (James keeps his in a green Bionicle canister), and then just leave them at Phil's house between sessions. This saves everyone the hassle of carrying ten pounds of change, but it does rely on the uncertain precept that Phil won't steal your money between poker nights.

If you want to start a new game with small change, go to a bank or a friendly merchant and buy some rolls of coins. Figure out how much everyone is likely to need, and get that amount in a mix of nickels, dimes, and quarters. Or, you can ask everyone to bring their own coins, but you should still be prepared to accommodate players who don't. For a nickel-quarter game, everyone probably needs about $10 in coins, with about $5 in quarters, $3 in dimes, and $2 in nickels.

Mike and James prefer chips. Chips are pretty, and they make a satisfying clicking noise, but the real reason to prefer them is that they are easier to count and handle than coins. In choosing chip colors, if you have that luxury, you can use whatever scheme you like. Here are two color schemes that make some kind of sense.

First, the "casino" color scheme. In most casinos, white chips are dollars, red chips are $5, greens are $25, and blacks are $100. From there up it's less predictable, and not every casino uses this scheme. At the Orleans in Las Vegas, for example, the dollar chips are brown. If you go to the cashier and ask for six racks of whites, which James has done, they will just giggle and stare at you. White chips are $500 each.

Amount	Casino Scheme	House Scheme
1 cent	White	—
5 cents	Red	White
10 cents	Blue	Red
25 cents	Green	Blue
100 cents	Black	Black
500 cents	Your choice	Actual money

You can divide the casino scheme by $100, which results in white chips being pennies, reds nickels, greens quarters, and black chips dollars. You probably won't need pennies, so you can use a different fourth color, often blue, for dimes. In addition, it helps if you have a fifth color for $5 or $10 chips, but you can also just use real bills for these larger amounts.

Next, the "house" color scheme. This is a more traditional coloring scheme for home games in which you assign the lightest chips the smallest value, and move up. So you might use white chips for nickels, reds for dimes, and blues for quarters. In a scheme like this, an eight-player game will need about 500 chips as follows: 300 white, 100 red, and 100 blue. Without chips larger than a quarter, you may need dollar bills.

Some poker chips are labeled with denominations like $1, $5, $10, and $25, but this can be distracting if you are not going to use them for exactly these denominations. In James's twice-monthly Wednesday night game, for example, pink chips are worth 17 cents, purple chips are worth 31 cents, and violet chips are worth 99 1/2 cents Canadian. This would be nearly impossible to remember if the chips had different denominations written on them.

Whatever their denominations, decent poker chips will cost you between 5 cents and 95 cents each. The cheap plastic chips from the dime store are about $5 for a hundred, but they are so light and slippery that you'll immediately wish you had something else. If these are your only choice, save your money and play with coins.

You should expect to pay about 25 cents each for a decent set of clay chips from a gaming supply store, or $25 per hundred. You can probably do better on the Internet or by hitting garage sales. For a game with eight players, you'll need about 500 chips (that's 200 of the smallest denomination and 100 of three other colors), which at 25 cents a chip comes to $125. It may seem ridiculous to pay 25 cents for a chip that represents a nickel, but a good set will last forever. Look for a weight between 8 and 11 grams, or the word "heavy" in the name. Or the word "free" in the cost.

Did we say "free?" Yes, we did. Here's a great way to get a set of free casino-quality chips: buy them from a casino. How's that "free," exactly? Well, once you're done with these chips, you can take them back to the casino and get your money back. You won't get that kind of deal from the game store. So, yes, in a sense, they're free. You've given the casino an interest-free loan (at least as long as the casino stays in business), and they've lent you a very nice set of chips. Everyone wins. Okay, the casino is not likely to see it that way—casinos have a particular aversion to the phrase "everyone wins"—so don't brag about this trick while you're pulling it. In fact, we expect they'll be mad at us for even suggesting it, which is why we now travel to Vegas under pseudonyms and carry clever spy gadgets and disguise kits.

The "free chips" trick may seem a little exceptional for a home game (do you really want $500 tied up in chips?), but it's exceptionally smart if you happen to be playing a private game in a casino hotel. Before your game, go to the cage and buy enough chips for the evening, and voila. You have been spared the embarrassment of lugging your chip case through airport security, and you have borrowed some darned fine chips to boot. Assuming you use the chips at their face value, you don't even have to cash anyone out at the end of the night. Just kick 'em out and send 'em to the cage. And this, friends, is the way we've played many private games in Las Vegas.

HOW DO I "BANK" THE GAME?

If you're using chips, you or someone you trust will be responsible for "banking" the game. This requires just a little bit of know-how and preparation.

The bank's basic responsibilities are to make sure everyone gets the chips he pays for, and that everyone cashes out correctly when they leave. Hopefully, everyone will bring small change so that they can help you cash them out, but you can't be sure of that. Having about $40 in small bills and coins on hand will make cashing out easier.

When the game begins, sell players their chips in reasonably-sized stacks, like $5, $10, or whatever the buy-in is. This is easier if you set up several stacks of $5 by copying one counted stack. Make one pile of chips, say 10 high, and then "copy" that pile by putting another stack next to it and leveling them. This is much quicker than counting to 10 over and over again. At the beginning, put as many of the smallest denomination chip into play as you can, so that players always have enough small change. When the case runs out of small chips, then you can get the bigger chips out of the box and let the players make change for each other.

After you have sold everyone their buy-ins, count the money you've collected and make everyone double-check their stack. If you make a mistake in setup, you must catch it now, or it will cost you at the end of the night. Put the cash into a safe place like the chip case, separate from any other cash you might be responsible for, such as the rent.

Note that, as the bank, you do not have to put your own cash into the box, and you can take chips from the case whenever you like. If it helps you track your winnings, you could buy in like everyone else. But at the end of the evening, whether you are ahead or behind, you will be making up the difference from (or putting the winnings into) your pocket. Putting cash into the bank when you buy chips from yourself is really a wasted step. Just be sure never to take more chips than you can pay for.

When a player leaves, he will probably cash out with an uneven sum (assuming he cashes out with anything at all). It helps keep the bank stocked with change to ask the player to make his chips into an even amount by adding change from his pocket, if he can. If he's cashing out $4.95, for example, it's a lot more productive for him to put a nickel on the pile and collect $5. On the flip side, if he cashes out with $5.05, you can hand him the odd nickel. Or you can encourage him to leave it as a tip for the house.

When everyone cashes out for the night, cash out the smaller stacks first. Have everyone count and stack their chips in such a way that it's easy for you to check their counts, and have them complete odd dollar amounts if they can. If you didn't pay for your own chips, the amount of money left in the box at the end of the night should match the amount you have won; or, the amount that the bank is missing should match the amount you have lost.

If you don't want players to play with cash on the table (say, hypothetically, you're playing in a hotel lobby in Columbus and the house detective is snooping around), then it's best to prohibit players from buying chips from each other. You can also use a ledger system. This system assumes you trust everyone in the game. When anyone buys chips, just mark their purchase on a ledger. At the end of the night, you can finally get out the actual money as you cash everyone out. In this system, have those players who lost money cash out first and pay you, so you then have enough to pay off the winners. Do all this while the house detective is getting coffee.

WHAT DECKS SHOULD I USE?

That's decks, plural. You need two decks going; that's why they come in 2-packs. Why? Because unless everyone in the game is

an excellent shuffler, every dealer will delay the game while he mixes the cards. And if everyone in your game is an excellent shuffler, are you sure no one is cheating?

Speaking of cheating, make sure your two decks have different backs. This makes cheating harder, and also prevents the hilarity when the decks inevitably get mixed together.

The point of using two decks is that you can save lots of time by having one player shuffle while another player deals. Because there's no scrutiny on the shuffler (another game is going on), it's best if a dealer doesn't shuffle his own deck. So, have the player to the left of the next dealer shuffle his cards, then have the current dealer cut the cards. You should use a "cut card," either a piece of colored plastic or an advertising card from the deck box. This card goes on the bottom of the deck when the dealer picks it up, so that he doesn't accidentally flash the bottom card.

As for cards, we recommend plain old Bicycle 808 and Bee Club Special decks, and not just because we own boodles of stock in the United States Playing Card Company. Actually, we don't, but these days we wish we did. All the American brands of playing cards—Aviator, Maverick, Hoyle, and so on—are manufactured by the Fine Folks at USPC.

If you think you're too hip to play with normal playing cards, you probably want to pick up an official Iraqi Most Wanted deck (how 2003!), or maybe that deck with the French ladies with very little French clothing, or maybe your special edition Sammy Sosa deck. See, on the 10 of Hearts, here's Sammy smiling! And here's Sammy hitting the ball! Here's Sammy smiling *and* hitting the ball! And on every card, here's Sammy obscuring critical game information, like what freakin' card it is.

See, custom card fronts can't be distinguished from more

than a few inches away. That doesn't make for very good poker. So, after you've shown off your Vive Les Smurfs deck, with entertaining portraits of every Smurf in history and four indistinguishable blue suits (Smurf heads, Smurf feet, Smurf fruits, and Smurf heads that face the other way), destroy that thing and break out the real cards.

One source of cheap, legible, and high-quality cards is, you guessed it, casinos. Most casinos sell their used decks to consignment houses for almost nothing, who in turn sell the cards into gift shops and drug stores. If you're lucky, your cards have been hand-sorted by an inmate in a Nevada correctional facility, perhaps even a compulsive gambler. Some of these decks are blackjack decks, which will mean (possibly) weird marks on the Aces and 10s. The best ones are poker decks, which look just right.

You should expect to pay about $1 each for used casino decks. One caveat: These decks will all be marked or cut to distinguish them as unplayable, so cheaters don't sneak them right back into the casino. Some canceling methods render the cards genuinely unplayable, since every card is marked or cut differently.

You should have at least two new decks for every game. That means you're kicking extra money into every game, but new cards do make for a much better game. It's nice to have a few backup decks, too. Despite the plastic coating and laminated cardstock in your new deck, bad shufflers will have little trouble bending those things up.

Once a card is smudged, bent, or otherwise unplayable, don't throw away the whole deck! Save the cards until another card from a matching deck is wrecked; chances are it won't be the same card. Keep those decks for when the four-year-olds come over to play Go Fish, or for your next marathon solitaire game, when the power is out and you are forced to play Klondike with real cards.

Whether your cards are new or old, always count the deck before you start the game. Otherwise you run the risk of doing what Mike did recently, —dealing a 3 of Spades to James and another 3 of Spades immediately to himself. Only the slightly different-sized numbers made it possible to tell that these two cards were from different decks. Oh, and deductive logic predicated on the fact that they were both 3s of Spades.

In addition to cards, you'll want a few other items to improve your gaming experience. Get something to serve as a "button," a large chip or other item that signifies who's dealing. (Yes, we know it's the guy with the deck in his hands, but really, sometimes it isn't.) For some games, you'll also need some markers called "legs" to designate partial victories. You'll need at least three per player; we like using actual sets of legs from Lego figurines, but only because we have hundreds of them. A few games in this book suggest a couple other necessities, such as a pad of paper or an egg timer. We'll make sure you know about those as they come up.

WHAT FOOD SHOULD I SERVE?

Like all vertebrates, your players must eat or die. Having each player bring their own personal chef will not do, since you presumably only have one kitchen. You should therefore provide some snacks to encourage them to leave their chefs at home. Consider the following options:

DRINKS: Soda and/or juice is required. Unless age or propriety precludes it, we also have some alcohol on hand, though we don't necessarily drink it. Some players find the Great Social Lubricant doesn't exactly improve their decision-making. But if your friends can handle their liquor (specifically, if they lose money at cards but don't seem to mind), you can be generous with the booze and they will pay you with their chips.

PIZZA: It's the classic party food, which you can usually get delivered to your door in fifteen hands or less. It's one of the few foods that's good hot and cold, and that's good, since it will exist in both states over the course of the night. And hey, some of your friends might even be resourceful enough to order it for themselves. However, nothing ruins a deck of cards faster than pizza grease (except, perhaps, a wood chipper), so you should have plenty of paper towels on hand and insist that people keep their pie away from your cards. If this means locking them in the kitchen, so be it.

DELI TRAYS: Even your carb-shy friends will have some options on the deli tray. Important safety tip: Keep the shrimp on ice if you want people to live.

CHIPS AND DIPS: Potato chips, popcorn, Funyuns, Chex Mix, and the like make for constant snacking, but each has its own level of intolerable grease. The pretzel bowl can move freely around the table, the Chee-Tos not so much.

APPETIZER BUFFETS: An upscale poker event can be catered with dim sum, tapas, petit-fours, or any other spread of trendy finger foods. The all-herring smorgasbord is a perfect choice. But if you even know what "petit-fours" means, you're way ahead of us. Handle it without our help.

DESSERT: Donuts yes, apple-bobbing no. (Donut-bobbing, absolutely.)

Things not to serve include chili (yes, that *Blazing Saddles* scene was funny, but not in your house), really heavy food, live eels, and fondue. Though playing cards around a flaming pot of tiny swords is entertainment, especially after midnight. Drunk.

WHO PAYS FOR ALL THIS?

Once you've decided what to serve, you must decide who's going to pay for it. Too often, Mike tells the story of five players gathering at a couple's house, where they served a couple of deli trays. To share the cost, the couple collected a "kitty"—a house rake of chips—by keeping each guest's dollar ante. At the end of two hours, the kitty had $300 in it. Man, those were some expensive deli trays.

Before you get too creative, decide whether you're running a game or a restaurant. It's fine to ask your guests to share the costs. It's quite another thing to sell them snacks at a profit. You already bought the poker chips and tricked out the poker table, so it doesn't hurt to spread out the weekly food costs. But be reasonable about it.

Here are some options: You can make it potluck, having one person bring snacks, another beer, and so on. You can collect a nominal contribution (a buck or two) from each player in advance—not afterwards, because someone may claim to have lost too much to pay, and not everyone will sympathize. In a regular game night, you can rotate the obligation, having one person bring the food on the 14th and another on the 21st. Or you can just be a grownup and repeatedly treat your friends to your down-home (read: extremely cheap) hospitality.

If you insist on collecting a kitty, aside from the fact that this may violate local gaming laws, consider this: If you spend $40 for food and you plan to play for four hours, you should collect $10 an hour. A hand of poker takes about two minutes, or thirty hands an hour. So you need to collect about 33 cents a hand. In a nickel-ante game with eight players, the ante that isn't yours is . . . 35 cents. Perfect! Explain the numbers like that, and people might not mind paying. But really, if you really want 5 bucks from everyone, why not just ask them for 5 bucks?

At Mike's house, the cost to walk in the door is 50 bucks. It seems like a lot for a nickel-quarter game. But remember, he's got some mighty excellent deli trays.

ANY OTHER ADVICE?

Yes. Clip your damn fingernails. Clean your house. Take out the garbage. Do the dishes. Scrub down the bathroom. Get extra toilet paper. Vacuum the rugs. If you want people to come to your place, make it so they enjoy being there, or at least aren't horrified.

Let people know what they are walking into when they come to your house. Do you have cats? Do you permit smoking? Are there small children? Is it impossible to park? Do you live under a bowling alley? Has your water been shut off? Can they see the house number from the street? Is there a security gate? Do all who enter have to offer a sacrifice to Ahura-Mazda? Let 'em know.

Finally, make sure you have your house rules in order. And make sure you, or one of your guests, know enough about poker to settle the disputes that will arise. This material is all covered in gory detail in Chapter Two, so do take the time to read it. Enjoy the concise and edifying commentary in Chapter Two while you can, because it's your last port of call before you hit the iceberg that is Chapter Three.

OKAY, THEY'RE HERE.
NOW WHAT?

Relax. A well-planned party takes care of itself. Invite everybody in, give them some drinks, cash them in, and move on to the dealer's choice section. There, we'll talk about how to play the most outrageous of poker games, and with luck you'll find a few that you actually like.

Chapter 2
THE BASICS

Following are the rules to the fundamental poker games, games that are too common to wind up in Chapter Three. While several common games are listed below, most games in Chapter Three are based on just three of them: Five Card Draw, Texas Hold 'Em, and Seven Card Stud. In fact, more than half of them are based on Seven Card Stud.

Later in the chapter we'll talk about such crucial concepts as shuffling, raising rules, and so on. For now, we'll start with the hands.

THE POKER HANDS

Here is the complete list of normal poker hands, in ascending order. Both cards and hands have "ranks," where those of lower ranks are beaten by those of higher ranks. Aces are abbreviated as "A," while Jacks, Queens, and Kings are "J," "Q," and "K."

If a hand contains more than five cards (for example, in Seven Card Stud), only five of the cards can be used in your hand. If the best five cards in different hands are identical, the hands are tied regardless of their sixth and seventh cards. This list can, of course, be altered by the dealer's call.

HIGH CARD: This is the worst hand, also called "no pair." A high card hand is often called "(high card) high," such as "Jack high." This hand is compared against other hands of the same rank by comparing the highest card first, then the next highest card, and so on. For example, K–9–8–7–2 beats Q–J–10–9–5. Aces are high for this purpose. Suit has no bearing when comparing poker hands, so a King of one suit is no higher or lower than a King of another suit. If all cards in both hands are of the same rank, the hands are tied.

ONE PAIR: Two cards of the same rank, such as Q–Q. When comparing two pairs of the same rank, compare the "kickers," which are the other cards in the hand, starting with the highest. For example, 6–6–Q–10–4 beats 6–6–J–10–9.

TWO PAIR: Two pairs, such as Q–Q–5–5. The higher of the pairs is compared first, so this hand is also referred to as "(higher pair) over (lower pair)." For example, "Aces over 6s" is A–A–6–6, and beats "Kings over Queens," or K–K–Q–Q. Sometimes, since the higher pair is so much more important, two pair is simply described as "(higher pair) up," such as "Kings up."

THREE OF A KIND: Three cards of the same rank, such as J–J–J, also called "trips." If two players have trips of the same rank, compare their kickers. (Two identical trips are possible in a game with wild cards, or in a shared-card game like Texas Hold 'Em.)

STRAIGHT: Five cards in numeric sequence. Aces can be used as high or low in straights, but not both, and straights are compared against each other by the rank of the top card in the sequence. In other words, A–2–3–4–5 is the lowest straight, 10–J–Q–K–A is the highest, and Q–K–A–2–3 is not a straight.

◆ *Nonstandard Hands:* A few games allow for nonstandard hands, such as the wrap-around straight, a straight that uses an Ace in the middle, the lowest being J–Q–K–A–2; the skip straight, which is a series of cards separated by one step, like 4–6–8–10–Q; or the blaze, a collection of any five face cards. The most common nonstandard hands are found in games played with three cards.

◆ *Why Does a Flush Beat a Straight?* The hardest thing to remember in the ranking of poker hands is whether a flush beats a straight. It's complicated by the fact that it's actually easier to draw to a flush than a straight, once you have four of the cards, since nine cards complete the flush and at most eight cards complete the straight. However, the rankings are based on the odds of being dealt the hand in the first place, and there are almost twice as many possible straights as flushes.

FLUSH: Five cards of the same suit, such as five hearts. Like high card hands, two flushes are compared on the basis of their highest cards first. Suit order is irrelevant.

FULL HOUSE: Three cards of one rank and two of another, also called a "full boat." The trips are compared first, so this hand is also referred to as "(trips) full of (pair)." For example, 10s full of 4s (10–10–10–4–4) beats 9s full of Jacks (9–9–9–J–J). In some situations, you might have to compare the pair as well. In this case 9–9–9–5–5 beats 9–9–9–4–4.

FOUR OF A KIND. Four cards of the same rank, also called "quads." When comparing two hands with quads of the same rank, compare the kickers.

STRAIGHT FLUSH: A hand that is both a straight and a flush: five cards of the same suit in sequence. The highest of these is 10–J–Q–K–A suited and is called a royal flush. Some lists describe a royal flush as a different hand, since they're so great, but it's just a very high straight flush. The royal flush is the highest hand possible without wild cards.

FIVE OF A KIND: This is the best poker hand, five cards of the same rank, and outranks a straight flush. It's only possible with wild cards, or some other wackiness.

In normal poker, straights and flushes are five-card hands. A three-card straight or flush is nothing. However, in a three-card game, such as Guts or 3–5–7, you may wish to include three-card straights and flushes. We don't advise it, since adding more hands doesn't really change the fundamental aspect of the game (unless you can draw cards, or receive them in sequence, which you rarely do in a three-card game). But if you do, be advised that the frequency of different hands changes with the number of cards dealt, so their rank order changes as well. A three-card straight flush is the best three-card hand, followed by trips, then a three-card *straight*, and then a three-card flush. All of these hands outrank a pair and high card, as you would expect.

HOW TO PLAY POKER

Plain ol' "Poker" is actually not a popular game. Nevertheless, it's a perfect starting point for the rest of this list, because it contains, in the most uninteresting way possible, the basic structure of most other poker games.

Poker requires a deck of fifty-two cards (no Jokers), and chips or money for every player. Each player antes a small amount, usually the smallest chip or coin, which means putting it in the center to become the basis of the pot, which is the amount to be won.

A dealer shuffles the deck and deals five cards to each player. Each player looks at his own cards.

There is now a betting round. The player on the dealer's left begins. The options are to: (1) check (bet nothing); or (2) bet any amount of money. That bet goes into the pot.

If the first player checks, the next player has the same choices. But if there's a bet, the next player may call (match the

---

♦ *Why "Four to the Ace" is Even a Rule:* Many houses play Five Card Draw with a rule that you can normally draw up to three cards, but you can draw four if you show an Ace. This is a meaningful rule with exactly six players, because it requires exactly fifty-two cards. The deck is exhausted if they all stay in, and they all take the maximum draw, including four players who draw four cards to a single Ace. Why the fourth player doesn't keep at least one card with the Ace is not clear. He certainly isn't going to pair his Ace.

Although this rule does allow more options than just drawing three cards, they're all the wrong options. The fact is that there aren't many times when the odds justify your holding onto one card in Draw, even if it's an Ace. However, it might be more interesting if Aces were wild....

bet), raise (increase the amount of the bet) if he desires, or fold (surrender the hand and drop out of the game). This process continues around the table until each player has contributed an equal amount to the pot or folded.

At this point there is a showdown. All live players (those who have not folded) show their hands, and the best hand takes the pot.

As you might have guessed, no one actually plays straight poker: there are no wild cards, no exposed cards, no drawing rounds, and only one round of betting. Basically, it's dull, dull, dull. But this seems to be where poker started. Pretty soon it evolved into a bunch of different animals, of which Draw, Stud, and Hold 'Em now dominate. But the betting structure, hand ranks, and look and feel of the game are the same.

FIVE CARD DRAW

Five Card Draw is best played with a small group, three to five players. With more than five players, the number of cards a player can draw must be limited, since there are only fifty-two cards in the deck. (If five players each discard and draw five cards, that's fifty cards all together). Typically in a six- or seven-handed game your draw is limited to four or to three cards, but basic Five Card Draw lets you draw as many as you want.

To begin, everyone puts a nickel (or other agreed amount) into the pot; this is called an ante. The dealer shuffles and deals five cards to each player. Starting on the dealer's left, players may bet, check, or fold per the rules of basic Poker.

After the first betting round, each player in turn, starting on the dealer's left, may discard and replace any number of cards. Players may also stand pat, drawing no cards.

Then, starting with the player who opened the pot (the player who made the first bet on the first betting round), or on

the dealer's left if there was no bet, a second round of betting takes place. After that betting round there is a showdown and the best hand wins.

VARIANTS: If there are six players, and everyone draws five cards, the deck will come up short. This rarely happens, but if it does the dealer (and possibly even his neighbor to the right) will be unable to draw. With six players it's best to limit the draw to three cards, or make the dealer sit out the hand. With seven players, you must limit your draw to two. With eight players, you probably shouldn't play Five Card Draw.

In some houses, the second betting round always begins on the dealer's left, regardless of who bet and raised on the first round. In other houses, the second round begins with the "last aggressive player," meaning the player who last bet or raised. You should make sure everyone's playing the same game.

In a few houses, the drawing restriction is lifted when enough players fold before the draw. For example, seven players may start with a drawing restriction of two cards, but when three people fold before the draw, the live players are allowed to draw as many as four. This will definitely change the way people bet, but if you want to play this way, you're allowed. Just make sure everyone is on the same page.

SEVEN CARD STUD

After people in groups of seven realized they were tired of only drawing two cards, they hit on a way to make the same seven cards work better, and simultaneously add three more betting rounds. "If we only get seven cards," they figured, "let's have all of them at once, and pick our best five at the end. Then everyone will have better hands and we can all win more money!" Or at least, that's how we imagine it.

Anyway, Seven Card Stud represents a major change from Five Card Draw, and descended by way of an endangered species called Five Card Stud. Because the Seven Card game is more prevalent and they're really very similar, we'll describe Seven Card Stud first.

After the ante, the dealer shuffles and deals three cards to each player as follows: two facedown "hole" cards, and then one faceup "board" card. There is a betting round starting with the highest board card. If there are multiples of that card, the betting starts with the "first" (i.e., closest to the dealer's left) high hand.

If a player folds, he turns all his cards face down and discards his hand. This helps the dealer remember who should still receive cards.

Three more rounds of cards are dealt faceup, one at a time, and then one more facedown, each round followed by betting. The player with the highest visible hand starts the betting each round. After the final betting round there is a showdown in which each player chooses any five of his seven cards to make the best hand.

Cards and their associated dealing and betting rounds are often named after streets. The first upcard is called "Third Street" in Seven Card Stud, because it's your third card (despite the fact that it's the first chance to bet, and might equally have been called "First Street"). Subsequent cards are called Fourth, Fifth, and Sixth Streets, followed by the final card, which is the "river." (We'll see this term again later.)

FIVE CARD STUD: Players receive a total of five cards, one down and four up. A betting round follows the first two cards, and every card thereafter.

SIX CARD STUD: This is rarely played but is a perfectly suitable Stud game if you feel like it. Cards are dealt 1-4-1, which means one card down, four cards up, and one card down.

EIGHT CARD STUD: Cards are dealt 2-5-1: two cards down, five cards up, and one card down.

RUNNING OUT OF CARDS IN STUD: You can play Seven Card Stud with eight or even nine players and never break a sweat. How so, asks your inner math genius? Won't the deck run out of cards?

Well, with fifty-two cards, a lot of people have to stick around for a long time for the deck to actually run out of cards. However, there is still the remote possibility, so you should do what the professionals do when, in the one game in a thousand, everyone hangs on until the end. It's called a community card.

If everyone stays in, the river card isn't dealt facedown. Instead, a single card is dealt into the middle of the table and can be used by all the players. It's scary, perhaps, that no one will get a secret seventh card. But hey, with all these opponents, you probably didn't stick around unless your first six cards were pretty good.

The important thing about this rule is just that you know it. Hold it in reserve for the one time when you need it, and then relax and play Seven Card Stud with a full table.

Why you should always stay for your last card in Seven Card Stud: With seven cards, you can make a total of twenty-one different hands. With only six cards, you have a total of six possible hands. And with five cards you can only make one five-card hand. What does this mean? That your sixth and seventh cards in Seven Card Stud are worth respectively, six and twenty-one times more than your fifth. Why *wouldn't* you pay to see them?

And if you believe that, we'd like to explain why most big numbers are even.

As specious as this little argument sounds, it's actually a good example of the kind of flawed logic that poker players use all the time. It's kind of entertaining to listen to career players try to convince you that hearts are the most common flush, or a 7-Deuce is the Texas Hold 'Em hand most likely to be paired on the flop. But you should take all their arguments, as well as ours, with a grain of salt. The fact is that the "seventh card logic" above is more or less the opposite of the truth. With two cards to come, you have far more possible hands than when you have received your seventh card. Poker strategy derives from knowing what proportion of the possibilities will be good for you. Not from listening to truck drivers talk about math.

With nine players, it's even possible that the deck will be unable to deal a sixth card to every player, if all nine players stay in on Fifth Street. The dealer should always count the deck before dealing Sixth Street just to be sure. Remember, you need to have enough cards left over to deal to all the players and still have a community card left at the end. If you don't, players will have to share Sixth Street as well as the river.

LOWBALL

Lowball is a contest for lowest hand, and you can do this in almost any game you care to play. Seven Card Stud is the most frequently played Lowball game (and is often called Razz). Playing for the worst hand isn't as simple as it sounds, however, since Aces might or might not be forced high, and since nowadays a lot of people don't want a straight to count against them for low.

Therefore, when you call a Lowball game, what exactly qualifies as the lowest possible hand is up to you, or, if the dealer doesn't mention it, to the house rules. The four definitions for lowest hand, in descending order of popularity, are as follows:

OPTION 1: THE WHEEL. Straights, flushes, and straight flushes don't count, and Aces are low. Thus, the lowest hand is "the wheel," which is 5–4–3–2–A, suited or not. This definition of low is prevalent in casinos and many home games. If you're stuck for an answer, pick this one. It makes split-pot games much more interesting.

OPTION 2: 7-5 LOW. Straights and flushes count as high hands, and Aces are only high. In this case, the best low hand is 7–5–4–3–2 (not all the same suit), which is called a "75" for short. This definition of low is played in a few casinos and some home games.

OPTION 3: 6-4 LOW. Same as 75, but Aces can be low. The best hand is therefore 6–4–3–2–A. This is played once in a while, but not much.

OPTION 4: 6-5 LOW. Aces are high, but straights don't count against you. In this case, the best hand is 6–5–4–3–2. As far as we know, this version is not used anywhere, but it completes the set. Who knows? Maybe you'll decide you like it.

◆ *Dead cards and low hands:* Dead cards are those cards that a particular game declares valueless. They are found in games like Socialism and Three Stooges, and can make for even lower hands than those described above. Those hands should still be ranked by the same basic principles that define the usual low hand (i.e., Aces high or low, straights and flushes counting or not). For example, if you have A–3–4–dead–dead, you will still need to know whether the Ace counts as high or low.

HIGH-LOW

In a High-Low game, the best and worst hands split the pot. Split-pot games are fun, because people tend to stay in for longer than they should. Still, splitting the pot between two or more different hands is a little tricky.

First, if the game is High-Low split, you need to define what qualifies as low. The four basic ways to do this are described under Lowball. If it is another type of split-pot game, such as Chicago, it's still important to know who qualifies for each half of the pot. For example, in Low Chicago, it's important to know that the Deuce, not the Ace, is the lowest spade.

Next, you must decide whether there will be a declaration round, an extra step at the end in which players simultaneously announce which half of the pot they will pursue, or sometimes both halves. A declaration round makes it impossible for a player to back into half of the pot by playing for the high hand only to discover that he has the low. It also makes it possible for a good guesser to win half the pot with a completely undeserving hand, simply by deducing that all other players will declare the other way.

Here's the process for a declaration round. Players take two chips below the table and return with a closed hand that holds either no chips (for low), one chip (for high), or two chips (for both ways). These chips are revealed simultaneously, so no one can change his mind at the last minute. Only players who went high will show down for high, and likewise for low. If you declare "both ways" you must win in both parts or you win in neither.

If no one goes for one half of the pot, the entire pot is handed to the winner of the side everybody declared.

If a player goes both ways and only ties for one of these categories, a fight will break out, involving at least one bloody nose and two people whose mathematical inadequacies will be laid bare for the world. This happens fairly rarely, but you'll need a definitive answer when it does. We believe the best solution is to count a tie as a win, and let the player take his fair share of both halves of the pot. We think he deserves this reward for taking the risk to go both ways. The other solution would be to say that if he doesn't win both ways outright, he gets nothing. But we think that's just cruel.

Most classic poker players believe in using the declaration round, rather than letting their cards speak, and it survives in games like Anaconda. Real old-schoolers even add another betting round after the declaration, in which the one fellow who went low raises the living daylights out of the three people who went high. But we think this extra betting round is a waste of time, so it's not standard in this book.

In many split-pot games, including Omaha-8 and Chicago,

a declaration round is not normally included. This means that the best high hand automatically takes half the pot, and the best other hand (in the case of Omaha-8, the qualifying low hand; in the case of Chicago, the high spade in the hole) takes the other half. If any players are tied, the pot is split appropriately; for example, if three players are tied for low, then their half of the pot is split three ways, and each gets 1/6 of the total amount in the pot. This, sadly, is usually less money than each put in.

High-Low Split games include High-Low Stud, Omaha-8, and Anaconda, and you can play just about any game high-low if you want. You'll know if you can't play a particular game for high and low because you'll get a creepy, sick feeling inside, and everyone at the table will swipe back their antes—don't try calling High-Low Rosencrantz and Guildenstern Meet the Three Stooges, unless you wish to play alone.

TEXAS HOLD 'EM

Currently, Texas Hold 'Em is a hugely popular game among amateur and professional players, and the most commonly played casino game in the United States. This will probably change in another ten years, as someone (perhaps even a game designer) comes up with something better. There are not a lot of variations on this game yet, perhaps because it's so young and sweet.

In Texas Hold 'Em, the role of dealer passes around the table, and the players on the dealer's left are obligated to "bet blind" before receiving any cards. This forced bet creates a pot and ensures that there will be no free rides on the deal.

Before the deal, the player on the dealer's immediate left must make a "Small Blind" bet, usually half the minimum bet. The player after him must make a "Big Blind" bet, equal to twice the small blind, or one minimum bet. (Blinds are fair only

> ◆ ***Three-Way Splits:*** If you ever invent a game with a three-way split, and you want a declaration round, it's quite simple. Use no coin for win 1 only, 1 coin for win 2 only, 2 coins for win 3 only, 3 coins for wins 1 and 2 together, 4 coins for wins 2 and 3, 5 coins for wins 1 and 3, and 6 coins for all three ways. Okay, just kidding. Actually, you need three coins of different colors, each corresponding to a different way to win, and players hold only those coins that represent the ways they are trying to win. In this case, holding no coins means you're folding. Go ahead and try it in your next game of High Chicago High-Low Split with a Declaration Round.

if everyone eventually has to pay them, so we suggest the dealer call an entire round of Hold 'Em, rather than one hand. It'll take less time than a single decent pot-matching game.)

Each player receives two downcards, and the first-round action begins to the left of the Big Blind. That player may fold, call the Big Blind, or raise. When the bet comes around to the Small Blind, that player may call (complete his bet and call any raises), raise, or fold. As his bet is "live," the player on the Big Blind has the option to raise when it's his action, even if his bet was just called. He can also call or fold as usual.

Next, the dealer deals three cards faceup in the middle of the table. These three cards are called the "flop." Cards in the middle are community cards, meaning that they are part of everyone's hand. Betting on this and subsequent rounds always begins with the player on the dealer's left; there are no mandatory bets after the first round.

After the flop, a fourth community card (the "turn") is turned up and a betting round follows. Then a fifth community card (the "river") is revealed, and the last betting round occurs. There is a showdown, in which each player makes his best five-card hand from the five community cards and the two cards in his hand.

Because of the low amount of information about specific players' hands, Texas Hold 'Em is a tough game to crack. You must glean what you can about a player's holdings by how he bets, whether he raises, and how he responds to your bets. For this reason, it's usually a good idea to make bets and raises in this game, because it gives you more information about other players' hands while giving them more chances to make mistakes. However, since a player's actions communicate his holdings, inexperienced players are harder to read than professionals, and even (in the short run) harder to beat.

It's a popular casino game these days for a few reasons. First, top players like it (especially when played no-limit) because it requires a lot of psychology and posturing, as well as a solid grasp of the math. Second, it's on television, so everyone who has cable has suddenly discovered that he's always wanted to play. And third, because the dealer spends less time dealing, she can deal more hands in an hour and bring in more money for the casino. So the casinos love it too.

BETTING NOTE: Many Hold 'Em games are structured, meaning that the only allowable bet and raise is the exact amount of the big blind in the first two rounds, and twice that amount in the next two rounds. The structure described above is no-limit, in keeping with the general principle of sidestepping bet structures in favor of explaining the basic rules. We recommend "spread limit," meaning that a player can bet or raise anything between the minimum and maximum bets of the table.

OMAHA AND OMAHA-8

Texas Hold 'Em has its own variants, the most popular of which are Omaha and Omaha-8.

Omaha is like Hold 'Em, with two changes: Each player has four cards, and must use exactly two cards from his hand

and three cards from the board to make his best five-card hand. This feels a little strange at first: You can be dealt four Kings and only be allowed to play two of them. (But hey, at least you know no one else has any Kings.)

Complain as you might about the "four Kings" problem, you still have many more potential hands in Omaha than you have in Hold 'Em. This reason, plus the fact that people play more hands than they should, means that the winning hands tend to be real whoppers. How many more options do you have? Well, in Hold 'Em, you can play both your cards with three from the board (that's ten different hands), one of your cards with four from the board (that's ten more), or you can play the board (that's unappealing option #21). In Omaha, you have six possible pairs of cards, each of which can be paired with three cards from the middle ten ways, for a grand total of sixty different hands. Unfortunately for the guy with four Kings, none of these sixty hands is four Kings.

"Omaha-8" is short for Omaha High-Low, with an 8 or better for low. The pot is split between the best hand and the lowest hand, but to qualify for low, your hand must be an "8 or better." What *this* means is that using two cards from your hand and three board cards, you must have five unpaired cards, the highest of which can be no higher than 8. Thankfully, straights and flushes don't count against you for low, and you can use different cards to make your high and low hands. The best low hand in Omaha is A–2–3–4–5, the "wheel." That's also a straight (for high), but a straight isn't that great when everyone has sixty possible hands. Also be aware that, because of the 8 or better qualifier, sometimes there's no low at all. For this reason, and the fact that it's much more likely to have to split the low with someone else, going for high is a better bet than going for low.

YOUR HOUSE RULES

When you set up your house poker game, you'll have to choose from a few of the options we described above, such as what (by default) is the lowest possible hand and whether, in Five Card Draw, you can draw four cards to an Ace. You will also need to address some other issues in this section, and it helps to make these rules available in writing to anyone who wants to see them. Luckily, we've made your life easier by presenting the rules you need, as well as a few collections of house rules to choose from. The terms in the rules are defined below.

PHIL'S HOUSE RULES

Game Format: Dealer's choice
Chips or Coins: Coins
Table Stakes: No
Buy-In: Any amount
Rebuy: Any amount, any time
Antes: Players ante a nickel
Minimum Bet: Nickel
Maximum Bet: Quarter (can be altered by dealer)
Minimum Raise: Amount of last raise
Raise Limit: No limit to number when heads up; three raises otherwise
Check Raise: Allowed
Default Low: 6-4 Low (A–2–3–4–6, unsuited)
Wild Cards in High Hand: Wild cards have no value alone
Wild Cards in Showdown: Can be any card
Midnight: The last game of the evening starts at midnight
Other Rules: The Edge is a valueless chip that serves as the ante for the player who won the previous hand; it does not count towards the pot value when doubling the pot, but can

count as a nickel when a pot is being split. Also, if a bet coin rolls across the table into another player's money well, the money goes to that player and the player who lost it must bet again.

MIKE'S HOUSE RULES
Game Format: Dealer's choice
Chips or Coins: Chips
Table Stakes: Yes, except for imbalanced games
Buy-In: $5 or $10
Rebuy: Any amount between hands
Antes: Dealer antes a nickel per player
Minimum Bet: Nickel
Maximum Bet: Fifty cents (can be altered by dealer)
Minimum Raise: Nickel
Raise Limit: No limit to number when heads up; three raises otherwise
Check Raise: Allowed
Default Low: The wheel (A–2–3–4–5)
Wild Cards in High Hand: Wild cards have no value alone
Wild Cards in Showdown: Can be any card
Midnight: Pot-matching games are only allowed after midnight
Other House Rules: Couples can't sit next to each other. And an Ace is always worth a dime. (Players at Mike's will "correct" a player who bets a nickel with an Ace showing by raising it to a dime.)

JAMES'S HOUSE RULES
Game Format: Dealer's choice (H.O.R.S.E., with or without wild cards)
Chips or Coins: Chips

Table Stakes: Yes

Buy-In: $20

Rebuy: $20 only if you have less than $20 on the table

Antes: Low card bring-in or blinds, as appropriate

Minimum Bet: Nickel

Maximum Bet: Pot limit (the amount in the pot)

Minimum Raise: Amount of last raise

Raise Limit: No limits to number of raises

Check Raise: Allowed

Default Low: The wheel (A–2–3–4–5)

Wild Cards in High Hand: Wild cards bet high

Wild Cards in Showdown: Cannot duplicate any card in hand (no five of a kind)

Midnight: After midnight, all nickels and dimes are removed, and betting limits become quarter-dollar

Other House Rules: Before beginning play, deal for seats. Each player gets a card, and players sit in card order from highest to highest; ties are broken in suit order (spades highest, then hearts, diamonds, and clubs).

DESCRIPTION OF HOUSE RULES LISTS: Despite our willingness to play at each others' houses, we have very different structures for how we play. Phil's house is loose and informal, Mike's is a bit more structured but encourages many weird games, and James doesn't want any of that nonsense on his watch.

GAME FORMAT: These are all "dealer's choice" houses. The deal passes to the left and each dealer can call any game. At James's house, though, the dealer can only choose from the "H.O.R.S.E." options: Hold 'Em, Omaha, Razz (Seven Card Stud Lowball), Seven Card Stud, and Omaha-8 (the "E" is for "Eight"). When the dealer picks a game, a full round of that game is played, and then a button moves and the next player picks a new game. James plays "real poker" because he believes in practicing for real money games, which he also plays a lot. And because he believes that candy is for little kids.

CHIPS OR COINS: It's up to you to decide whether to use poker chips or coins in your home game. If you use chips, one player (usually the house) must play the role of banker, and ensure that all the chips are bought back correctly and that the bank is balanced at the end of the night. Mike and James like doing that, Phil not so much.

TABLE STAKES: This means several things at once: a player is only allowed to bet with the money he has on the table; he can't be put out of the hand by being outbet; and if he does go all-in (runs out of money in the middle of a hand), he is not out of the hand. Instead, all subsequent bets go into a side pot in which this player has no share. The side pot is contested in the showdown only by those players who have invested in it; after that, all players including the all-in player may show down for the main pot. A player may put more money on the table between hands in a table stakes game, but not in the middle of a hand. He can only remove money from the table when he cashes out for the night, except to tip the waitress, assuming she ever comes by.

The other option is "out of pocket," which Phil plays. To track money you are betting but not immediately producing, it's convenient to "drag light," moving chips from the pot to build up a pile which represents your further obligation to the pot. If you win, the debt is erased. If you lose, the total amount in front of you represents the amount you still owe the winner. If the pot is split, and you win half, you simply hand the marker stack to the other winner, and then split what remains down the middle.

Table stakes works until you start playing imbalanced games, which means any game in which players put different amounts into the pot. In a game where Aces cost an extra nickel, or catching a 5 makes you match the pot, it's infeasible and sometimes impossible to create an equitable side pot when a player goes all-in. Since Mike plays a lot of imbalanced games, he allows players to play out of pocket for those games only. While ludicrous in a casino, this is perfectly reasonable in a small-stakes home game. (Another way to do this is to say that if your table stake runs dry, you are always in for the whole pot, but have no power to raise the bet. You can still buy as many chips as you wish between hands.)

BUY-IN: This is the amount of money players can put on the table to start with. It really only matters in table stakes games, especially those with high betting limits, and it totally falls to pieces when you let players put more money into play in the middle of a hand. Mike and James use chips, so it makes sense for them to set buy-ins; Mike's buy-ins are set so making change is much easier. At Phil's, they play with nickels, and players can put whatever they want on the table. In amusing containers, if possible.

REBUY: Especially important in a pot-limit game, limiting the amount of chips players can buy keeps players from tabling too much money at once. At James's game, players can rebuy only when the chips on the table amount to less than $20.

ANTE: All these games are nickel ante, usually with each player anteing a nickel into each pot; this is called player ante. However, at Mike's game the dealer antes for everyone in the hand. The reasoning behind dealer ante is that the dealer may call a game that favors him, so it feels fairer for him to seed the pot for his own game. The net cost to everyone is the same, except when players constantly get up and sit down, thus changing the amount each dealer has to ante. In dealer ante, it's not permitted to skip your deal; in a player ante game, you can pass the deal at will.

At James's, all games have blinds or a "bring-in." This is a minimum bet on the first round that must be posted by a certain player, such as the one with the lowest upcard. (Ties are broken in suit order: clubs are highest, then diamonds, hearts, and lastly spades.)

MINIMUM AND MAXIMUM BETS: Phil's and Mike's are capped at 25 and 50 cents, but James allows players to bet the amount in the pot. These rules can be superseded by dealer's choice rules. For example, a usual bet limit of 25 cents doesn't prevent the dealer from charging players extra for wild cards.

All the prices in games in this book are set with a nickel-quarter game in mind. If you play at different limits, you should alter the prices accordingly. For example, in Low Hole Wild, the price is 50 cents (ten small bets) to get your last card face-up. If you play in a $6-$60 game, you can charge the player $60 for the privilege.

MINIMUM RAISE: In a casino environment with raise limits, players are not allowed to "eat up a raise" by making a tiny raise on top of a big one. For example, two players with great hands might raise $50, and the next player, less certain of success, might want to kill the last raise by raising the minimum of $5. In some house games like Mike's, that kind of micro-raise is allowed. James and Phil set theirs like most casinos, where the minimum raise for the current betting round is equal to the amount of the last bet or raise, but this drops back to the minimum bet at the start of the next round.

If the game is pot limit, the maximum bet is equal to the amount in the pot. This is fairly straightforward. The maximum raise is also equal to the amount in the pot, including the bet, which can be just a little more confusing. To do the math correctly, when you raise, think of it as two steps. Your call adds to the pot, which then increases the amount you can raise. For example, if there is 50 cents in the pot, and the bet is 10 cents to you. You can raise 60 cents, because you are first calling the 10-cent bet, then raising the 60 cents now in the pot.

None of the house games above are no-limit, but that structure is perfectly acceptable, too. In no-limit, there is never a maximum bet or raise. It's good to play no-limit games as table stakes, which means you can't bet more that you have on the table, and with a limited rebuy (such as, only rebuy for $10, and only when your chips are under $10). A dealer may choose to call a game with a pot limit or no-limit betting structure even in a nickel-quarter dealer's choice game, if the house rules allow for it.

RAISE LIMIT: This is the maximum number of raises allowed per betting round. This doesn't include the original bet, so one bet can be followed by as many as three raises. Raise limits are intended to prevent two players from infinitely raising a third player; in most houses, when the game is down to two players heads up, those two can raise each other as many times as they want. If you want to get technical, the round isn't actually heads up unless it begins with only two live players. In James's house, though, players are never limited in the number of raises they can make.

CHECK RAISE: This is something that all our houses permit, but yours might not. A check-raise means checking, then (if there is a bet) raising the bet on the same betting round. It's considered rude and dishonest in some old-fashioned houses, but it's also considered a crucial element of modern poker, and is allowed and encouraged in card rooms virtually everywhere. Poker is, after all, a game featuring a good measure of rude and

IF YOU REGULARLY PLAY POKER IN LAS VEGAS, YOU MAY NOT REALIZE THAT YOU **CAN** HAVE A SUCCESSFUL GAME IN YOUR HOME WITHOUT THE FOLLOWING:

dishonest behavior, which helps single it out worldwide as a distinctively American pastime.

DEFAULT LOW: Because a lot of games are high-low or straight low, it's good to have a house definition of low; Mike and James prefer the wheel, whereas Phil thinks straights are, well, straights and thus prefers 6–4. Any dealer can alter this low, but you must have a house rule to cover the times when the dealer forgets to specify. See Lowball for the four possible low hands and the ground rules that govern them.

WILD CARDS IN HIGH HAND: There's no telling where we picked this up, but in Mike and Phil's games, a wild card alone (or multiple wild cards with no naturals) doesn't qualify you to open the betting, so in a game like Seven Card Stud with Deuces wild, A–K will open the betting against 2–2. Weird, yes, and we can't find it anywhere in the literature. Nor can we really offer a good theoretical explanation of it. Phil's rationale is that the wild card acts like a catalyst in a chemical reaction; it affects other cards, but it has to have other cards to act off *of*. This sounds good enough to shut down pointless arguing at the table, except when the chemists drop by, and it's not like five wild cards isn't great in the showdown. In fact, it helps the wild card hand to not have to lead the betting, so maybe this rule was invented to give an edge to someone who really doesn't need it. But somehow we've picked it up. The alternative and more reasonable rule is that wild cards make the best possible hands, and 2–2, being thus a pair of Aces, clearly opens the betting against A–K.

WILD CARDS IN SHOWDOWN: In most houses, you can make a wild card into anything, which allows for things like five of a kind and a double-Ace-high flush. But James's house plays the old-fashioned way: You can't make a wild card into a card you already have. This means five of a kind is impossible, as well as the double-Ace flush, but when you're trying to make most other hands, the wild cards are just as good as ever.

One more clarification you will need to make concerning wild cards in the showdown is whether a natural hand, one made with no wild cards, is superior to the same hand made with wild cards. This comes up so rarely that most people don't bother having a rule for it, but you'll be happy if you do. We think both hands should be equal. But if you want the natural hand to prevail in the case of a tie, make it a firm house rule. (And be sure to state whether a straight using two wild cards for the low end loses to the exact same straight using only one wild card, but for the high end. See why we don't like this rule?)

MIDNIGHT: These are all rules for when the game will end, even if they don't look like it. Phil's kids will get him up at 7 A.M., so he calls the last game at midnight. James raises the stakes at midnight, increasing the bets to where only a few players will want to play. Mike says pot-matching games aren't allowed before midnight, which means that shortly thereafter, a lot of money will move into a very few pockets and everyone else will want to leave.

OTHER HOUSE RULES: You will probably find yourself adding a few more rules to your own list. Whatever they are, make sure they are fair and that everyone knows them. For example, if you want to encourage everyone to bring food, that's a good thing to spell out. If you don't allow pot-doubling games, or 3–5–7 in particular (because of that night when you lost $300 and you don't want to talk about it), let everyone know. The best thing about throwing your own game is that you get to set the rules. Just don't drop them on your players without warning, and don't be unfair. "Dave Always Wins" isn't going to go over very well, whether it's produced in writing or not.

SOME RULES NEVER CHANGE

Aside from the mostly-variable rules above, here are a few other ingredients we recommend as part of any set of house rules:

SHUFFLING: You probably shouldn't worry about cheaters in your house game, but just for fairness any player should be allowed to shuffle the cards before they are dealt. Typically, the dealer shuffles his own deck, then offers it to the player on his right for the cut. That player cuts the cards towards the dealer, breaking off at least a quarter of the pack and setting it on the table by the dealer. The dealer then completes the cut.

When a second deck is in circulation, it's even easier for a cheater to make his own deck while no one is looking, so we suggest that players shuffle the decks that will be dealt by the players on their right. Also, make sure your two decks don't have the same back. You would have thought of that as soon as you got started, we know.

If you're no good at shuffling, you should learn. The easiest shuffle, an overhand shuffle doesn't mix the cards up very well. A

riffle shuffle, the kind where you split the pack in half and then riffle them together (several times) is usually preferred, though professional dealers precede the riffle with a "scramble," a seemingly childish method of mixing the cards by spreading them all over the table. This is, like it or not, the best and fastest way to really randomize the pack.

This isn't really a book about how to shuffle and deal cards, so we'll leave it at that. If you're concerned about cheaters, you are playing with the wrong group. But you can take a look at *Scarne on Cards* for a great rundown on how cheaters cheat, and how you can, just maybe, catch them.

MISDEALS: There are two kinds of misdeals: harmless ones and the other kind. If the dealer isn't finished giving everyone cards, and he screws up in some unfixable way, anyone can call a misdeal and the game can restart. It's impolite, though strangely satisfying, to incorrectly call a misdeal just because you don't like your hand. The dealer will ignore you.

One common misdeal is when the dealer flips over one of the player's first two down cards in seven card stud. Luckily, this is fixable. The flipped card becomes that player's first upcard, and the dealer deals very slowly and carefully the next time around, giving the player another downcard when he's dealing everyone else's card up.

If the dealer screws up once the betting has begun, it's another story. Unfortunately, you probably don't have a floorman to call over and solve your problems, so the group needs to work out an equitable solution like adults. Here are the guidelines: If the dealer's mistake hurts only the dealer, it stands. If it hurts any other player, the solution should allow for the least possible damage to all players concerned.

An example: The dealer deals a player's last stud card face up. This hurts that player and helps everyone else, so the player is given the option to keep the card or get a new card face down. If the latter, the misdealt card is burned (discarded facedown).

Another example: The dealer begins dealing the next round before the betting on this round is complete. In this case, giving the players the choice to keep their cards unfairly helps them; the best solution is to shuffle the misdealt cards back into the pack, finish the betting, and then deal the round properly. You'll find some players who don't want the pack shuffled, an extra card burned, or anything else to happen to the order of the deck once the game begins, because they think this will deprive them of "their" cards. Probability theorists say that, until they are revealed, the cards in a shuffled pack don't have an order anyone can divine, so reshuffling the pack doesn't hurt anyone. But if these players can't be convinced, you may have to find a solution that doesn't involve reshuffling the deck. Like sending them to college.

STRING BETTING: String betting is the kind of betting they do in the movies. The handsome old cowboy says "I'll see your five dollars," and then takes a long slow drag on his cigar, scratches his eye, looks at his pet monkey, and after an interminable pause during which all eyes are fixed upon him, continues, "and I'll raise you five hundred." Put this cowboy in a real casino, and a cute young dealer will politely tell him to take back his raise.

Technically, here's what he did: He made a play that looked like a call, reached back for more money, and then announced his raise. This is a "string bet," so called because you're trying to string two actions into one. And it's not legal.

By apparently only calling, you are (so the theory goes) trying to get a reaction out of the next player, so you can judge the quality of his hand without actually making your raise. This behavior is really pointless in nickel games because, more than likely, the next guy doesn't even know that he's next, and he's certainly not going to give you any information about his hand while you puff your cigar.

But string betting is definitely not allowed in higher limit games, so it's good to get out of the habit while the stakes are low. String betting is a faux pas in a casino game, where the other players will slap you in the head for it. Yes, they actually get up and walk around the table and slap you in the head. No, really, they just brutally gang up and win all your money.

So, when you want to raise, just put all the money out at once so people can see what you're doing, or (even better) say "raise," and then take all the time you want.

SPLASHING THE POT: Some players just chuck their chips into the center. This angers some others, because it's difficult to tell whether the player actually put in what he said he did. So don't do it. Put your bet chips in a stack in front of you, and move it into the pot when everyone has called.

CARDS SPEAK: This is another universal rule that was not always universal. Time was when a player might say "flush!" when he missed seeing his full house, and he'd be held to his declaration of "flush," if in fact he had one. Nowadays, the cards speak for themselves, which means if you have any chance of misreading your hand it's better to show it to everyone, and let the rest of the table help you. (Around Phil's house, we refer to this as playing the game "Is This Good?") Another good reason to show your hand instead of throwing it away is that, if you surrender your cards when your opponent miscalls his hand (he announces he has a straight but he only has a pair), you now have no cards to beat him with, and must resort to using your fists.

SPLIT-POT DISCREPANCIES: When a pot is split, either because two people tied for the best hand, or because the game actually calls for a split pot, there may be an odd nickel. A few houses leave this odd amount in the next pot, but most people have a rule for where it goes.

If the game was split high-low, the odd nickel goes to the high hand. Similarly, if the game is best hand vs. "other hand," i.e., the high spade in Chicago, the best hand takes the odd nickel.

If two players split the pot by having identical hands, then the nickel is harder to assign. The casino's rule, and thus the one we suggest, is to give the odd coin to the earlier position, i.e., the first player on the dealer's left. This is supposedly the worse position, though in a dealer's choice game that distinction is completely arbitrary.

This is a whole lot of wrangling over a bit of small change, so it wouldn't hurt to add your own whimsical house rule that sends odd nickels out the window or into the beer fund. Just make it clear what happens so the game can continue without fisticuffs.

IF NO ONE WINS: Some dealer's choice games can result in no winners. The classic case is Jacks or Better, which is Five Card Draw with the requirement that you need Jacks or Better to open the pot, and the caveat that if no one opens the betting, the game ends. Unfortunately, there's still a pot in the middle. The rule in this situation, which has become the default for all such situations, is that the players re-ante and the game is redealt, with the pot carrying over.

The question at this point is, if everyone is to re-ante and the game is to be redealt, which players are actually in? There are actually three cases to consider: those in which no one dies, those in which some people die, and those in which everyone dies.

In the first case, as with Jacks or Better, everyone stays in because no one has been knocked out. All players can re-ante and the game can be redealt.

In the second case, some players have folded before the game is over, but some players were alive at the showdown. We prefer to allow only those players who were alive at the show-down to play the game again. This is usually enforced by the phrase "if you fold, you're out for good" in a game like Diablo.

In the third, since everyone has been killed, we would either have to step back until there were still some people in, and play the game again with just those players, or invite every-one back in. This is the case with a game like Good Cop, Bad Cop, in which an unlucky draw can knock everyone out. In this situation, we like to allow all the original players to re-enter the game. These games are crazy enough; they aren't hurt by this rule. You might even be more inclined to fold early and keep your fingers crossed.

Many games in this book have so many redeals that it's appropriate to use a dealer marker called a button to signify who acts first on each game. The button starts on the dealer and moves to the left with each deal. The action starts on the button's left.

ADDRESSING POSITIONAL ADVANTAGE: In casino-style Texas Hold 'Em, the player to the dealer's left always acts first, except on the first betting round, where he's been forced to post a blind bet. This puts him, arguably, in the worst seat at the table. The dealer acts last on every round, which puts him in the best seat. The dealer has the "positional advantage" of knowing everyone else's play before he has to act. This imbal-ance is acceptable in any game that stays the same all night, because the role of dealer rotates, and everyone sits in the hot seat the same number of times. When a new player enters the game, he's forced to post a blind, so he pays as much as every-one who's already there, even if he happened to sit down in a good position.

In a dealer's choice game, however, the advantage is always changing. One dealer might call No-Peekum, a game where, traditionally, the dealer has a howling disadvantage. The next player might call Diablo, a game where the dealer has the best · seat, though not by much. If you were trying to win consistently, you'd call only games that favor the dealer, and you'd sit out of games that aren't at least fairly balanced for your seat. But then your friends would never invite you over to play cards again.

What we'd rather do is root out the games that have more than a negligible positional advantage, and fix the problem if we can. We'll bring this up again throughout Chapter Three.

Stud games fix the problem almost completely, by making the high hand lead the betting. This favors players in later position only when hands are tied, because the hand closest to the dealer gets first action. We try to borrow this kind of randomized positional advantage whenever we can, so for example, in No Peekum we suggest you let everyone roll one card to start the round, and assign a leader based on that card.

But in a game like Hold 'Em, where a player's cards are never shown, the positional advantage is a tough nut to crack. We suggest you solve this by allowing the dealer to call a full round of Hold 'Em (complete with blinds) so that everyone gets a chance at every seat.

In pot-doubling games like Heinz 57, position can kill you. When a player gets a faceup wild card he must match the pot or fold. Players in later positions have more information when they get their wild cards, but this advantage can pale in comparison to the price they have to pay. One solution to problems like this is to deal all rounds after the first by starting with the high hand showing. This doesn't fix the problem completely, but it does a lot to balance the positions.

FOLDING OUT OF TURN: It's bad to do anything when it's not your turn, but it's especially problematic when you fold.

Even if you know you can't win, you will give extra information to other players if you throw your cards away before the action comes to you. While this is simply bad manners in a normal game, it can actually be ruinous in several dealer's choice games, because in these games one player's fold can steal the game away from a second player, and hand it to a third.

For example, in Countdown, the wild card is equal to the number of players. If one player folds out of turn, another may know his wild card has become unwild, or vice versa. This gives him extremely useful information about the outcome of the game. It's especially bad if it happens during the showdown. So we forbid it entirely.

Where we can, we've specifically pointed out when a game's outcome can be changed by an out-of-turn fold, and we always restrict players to fold only when the action is on them. In games like Countdown, we even require that the player owe money before he is allowed to fold, meaning that if the action is on you and there is no bet, you can't drop out.

WHO MUST SHOW THEIR CARDS: In nearly every circumstance, players are happy to show their hands at the showdown. If one player shows a good hand, and no one can beat it, the other players can throw theirs away. But if players are being snarky, there may come a moment when no one is willing to turn his cards over first. Perhaps neither player has a legitimate hand and they both fear the embarrassment and humiliation of being caught in a bluff. What these players don't realize is that they should be *more* willing to show their bluffs than their legitimate hands, since it will only convince other players that they play stupid cards all the time.

Good poker or not, this situation can arise. The solution is this: if there is a last aggressive player (the player who bet or raised last on this round) that player must show first. He's technically the player who "was called" by everyone else. If there is no such player, because the last betting round was checked around, then the obligation to show goes to the first player on the dealer's left.

In casinos, any player may ask to see a called hand (a hand that is live at the showdown) if collusion or cheating is suspected. The dealer kills the hand, if the player folded it, and then reveals it. But in most cases, once a player is beaten, he can throw away his cards facedown and no one cares.

In a situation when the players are all-in before the end of the hand, casinos require that all players reveal their cards before the deal continues. This also prevents collusion, and it makes good television, especially when the players stand up and holler obscenities and hike up their pants. They do this to relieve stress, because there are thousands of dollars at stake. Choose to behave like this with similar requirements in mind.

Now that you've gotten the basics down, we're going to change everything. The next chapter is the bulk of the book, the games you can call when the deal's on you. Most refer back to this chapter, so if a game says "Seven Card Stud," refer to the rules above for that game.

In this section you will find almost all the strange poker games we could cobble together. They are gathered from our home games, traditional resources, friends, our own tiny brains, and Phil's massive list of mutant poker games, which he's compiled over 25 years of playing for nickels. Phil has actually been playing for nickels since they were worth something, and we thank him for it. Some of these games are old favorites, and a lot are games you've never seen before. Some are exceptional games, some aren't worth playing even once. But we'll try to warn you if they're that bad.

First, under the name of each game you'll read exactly what the dealer would say when calling the game. If this description requires any further clarification, it is listed next. Then you'll find anything else about the game that we thought was interesting. Some descriptions are quick, some require much more detail.

As you will see, we like to make up games. You can do this too, of course. Just make sure your group is cool with playing a game that's still in "testing mode." Honestly, if they'll play all the games in this book, they're crazier than we are.

When we are talking about money values in these games, such as buying a card for 50 cents, we're assuming you're playing in a nickel-quarter game, where the ante is a nickel and the biggest bet is a quarter. You can adjust these values to whatever range is right for you, and always be sure to specify all these numbers whenever you call a game.

And now, let's put the cards in the air.

ACES WILD

Any game. Aces are wild.

CLARIFICATION: A "wild card" can become any card you want, even a card you already hold. In some houses, peopled mainly by the star attractions from *Jurassic Park*, a wild card can't be made into a card you already hold. This rule makes impossible hands like five of a kind, and a double-Ace-high flush. However, unless you say differently, a wild card can be made into any card.

BACKGROUND: This concept makes this book possible. We think it likely that the first cards affected were the scorned Deuces, instead of the valuable Aces. One can see some mule skinner grimly staring at yet another pair of ducks and his poke melting away to the Kansas City dandy across the table. As he folds, he proposes that the "damned Deuce" be made "wild," like getting a king in checkers. It's an amusing enough idea that the others agree, and lo and behold our mule skinner gets his double ducks again, this time with two Treys. When the Kansas City sharp reveals his full house, the skinner grins and spreads his four of a kind on the table. And because he's a *smart* jasper, the sharp gets a bullet in him before his silver-plated derringer has cleared his sleeve. The skinner collects his money and spreads his magic out into the world. The slippery slope leading to Frankenstein, Diablo, and Schrödinger's Cat has begun.

VARIANTS: "Something's wild" is pretty much the safest game to call if you've never played dealer's choice before. Popular variants include *Deuces Wild* (2s are wild), *7-Up* (7s are wild), *Ladies' Night* (Queens are wild), and *One-Eyed Jacks and the Man with the Axe* (the Jack of Hearts, the Jack of Spades, and the King of Diamonds are wild). Our house has a game called

Philsbane, which is simply "4s are wild," a fact that Phil managed to forget three times in one night. Hence, Philsbane.

Expect the winning requirement to go up by about one hand rank (such as from two pair to trips) for every two wild cards in the game. So it's important to know how many wild cards there are: In Aces Wild, there are four wild cards. If it's One-Eyed Jacks, there are only two. If it's Jokers, it's two cards out of fifty-four, just slightly fewer than two in fifty-two. A game with a wild suit, such as *Redball* (diamonds are wild), gets you thirteen wild cards. And if some character calls "All red cards wild," then there are twenty-six wild cards in the game. If you have called only one wild card, such as the Suicide King, whoever gets that card will have a pretty big advantage.

Sometimes you'll want conditional wild cards; these usually require additional rules. For example, in the game *Foundation*, Aces are wild, but if you have an Ace, then your 2s are wild; if you have an Ace and a 2, your 3s are wild; and so on. In games like this, your wild cards can't enable other wild cards; that is, if you make an Ace into a 2, it doesn't make your 3s wild. You can squelch all debate by throwing in the word "natural," meaning having the rank or suit in question printed on the card. So in Foundation, if you have a natural Ace, your 2s are wild.

We have a house game called *Jane Austen*, in which 2s and 3s are wild. There's no justification for this name, except that Jeff (the player who "invented" it) thinks it's ironic that there's no justification for it. You'll be hearing a lot about our friend Jeff. He's a math genius who's fond of terrible games like Good Cop, Bad Cop, mostly because he enjoys watching the suffering of others. He's eager to point out that wild cards aren't "wild," since they always become the best possible card. If they were really "wild," he argues, they might turn into anything! So, he prefers to call them "controlled."

ONE MORE NOTE ABOUT PLAYING WITH JOKERS:
If you don't normally play with the Jokers in the deck, adding them back into a used deck can be a mistake. The Jokers will have glorious white edges, while the rest will be gray. Anyone looking at the side of the pack can see immediately where the Jokers are. So please, if you're going to play with Jokers, make sure you have a new deck where they don't advertise themselves.

♦ *Games That Aren't Poker: ACEY-DEUCEY*

There are plenty of games that aren't poker. Charades isn't poker. Neither is dodgeball. But we've decided to cover a few particular games in this book because, despite only a passing similarity to real poker, they are played way too much at dealer's choice poker games. Acey-Deucey is a prime example. There are no hands, no rounds of betting, and no bluffing. Dealers tend to call it as a "break" between poker games, and hey, everyone has got money on the table, so we might as well play. Or we might as well go to the kitchen for one of those yummy peanut butter brownies.

Also known as *Between the Sheets*, Acey-Deucey is a game you play against the "house" (basically, against the deck), and not against each other. To create a reasonable sized pot, everyone antes 25 cents. Before dealing, the dealer exposes a card and puts it faceup on the bottom of the deck. He then addresses each player individually. Starting with the player on his left, the dealer turns over two cards in the center of the table, leaving space for a third card between them, and asks the active player to make a bet. The player's bet can be anything from zero to the amount in the pot, though on the first round the maximum bet is half the pot.

If the bet isn't zero, the dealer turns over a third card between the first two. If its rank falls between the first two cards, the player wins, and takes the amount of his bet out of the pot. If the card is outside the range, the player loses, and pays his bet to the pot. If the card is the same as one of the outside cards, he must pay double his bet.

Neighbors and Pairs: If the first two cards are neighbors, such as 7–8, the bettor can't bet. Instead, he is "burned" and forced to pay a nickel. If the first two cards are a pair, the bettor is burned for a dime.

Aces: The first Ace dealt to a player can be either high or low, at the player's option. The dealer must ask the player to call the Ace high or low before dealing the second card. The second Ace is always high, so it's usually safer to call the first Ace low. A low Ace and a high Ace aren't a matched pair, but an Ace as the third card matches one of them for sure.

Ending the Game: The game ends when someone takes the last coin in the pot. If the dealer exhausts the deck, the last card isn't played. Instead, any cards that have been exposed on this round remain on the table, and the rest are shuffled and made into a new deck. There is no burn card on the second and later deals.

STRATEGY: Really, the only good strategy in Acey-Deucey is deciding not to play. It's also a terrible game from a design standpoint for any number of reasons, including positional advantage, wrenching futility, and immense volatility. Then again, this must be what people like about it, as they've penned variations that accentuate all three.

Still, position matters only if you're paying attention: The players who act later in the round have more information about what remains in the deck, as long as they have some method of keeping count. A safe bet on a new deck requires that the first two cards be separated by no less than 8 ranks (such as 2–10) to get a positive expectation. But players typically make small bets with shorter gaps to keep the game "interesting." Strictly speaking, if it's worth betting a nickel, it's worth betting the pot, but as with most games with simplistic strategy, playing smart only takes away the fun.

VARIANTS: According to a singularly amazing guest at one of Phil's poker nights, here's the way they play Acey-Deucey in Philadelphia. In *Acey-Deucey with Wide Goal Posts*, if your middle card neighbors either of the first two, even on the inside, you lose double your bet. (Note: A King is not a neighbor of a low Ace.) This means that the only spreads with a positive expectation in a fresh deck are A–Q, A–K, 2–A, 3–A, and A–A. Every other bet is, on average, a loser. We can only assume that when poker gets boring in Philadelphia, they just go outside and hit each other with shovels.

ADDITION

Seven Card Stud. A player may combine any cards from ranks Ace through 9 by adding their ranks into a single card of rank 10 or less. If all the combined cards are of the same suit, the new card retains that suit; otherwise, the new card is unsuited and cannot be used in a flush.

CLARIFICATION: Here's an example. A 3 of Spades and an Ace of Spades can be combined to make a 4 of Spades, or they can be combined with a 4 of Diamonds to make an 8 with no suit, assuming you want two less cards.

VARIANTS: Math guys like Jeff insist on playing this game with new mathematical formulas. Their eyes are, almost always, bigger than their stomachs. In *Subtraction*, a player may subtract one or more cards of rank 10 or less from another such card to make an existing card. In *Multiplication*, you can multiply one card times another to make another card of 10 or less (you'll need a 2 or 3 for sure). In *Division*, you can do the reverse of what's in Multiplication, and also divide a number card by another card of the same rank (i.e., sacrifice a pair) to make an Ace. If you want to play *Square Roots, Primes, Perfect Numbers, and the Fibonacci Sequence*, you're on your own, genius.

AFGHANISTAN

Seven Card Stud. It costs a quarter to open, and a dollar to fold. If no one opens, all players re-ante and a new hand is dealt.

CLARIFICATION: The minimum opening bet is a quarter. This doesn't mean that it costs an additional quarter on top of your opening bet, though you could call it that way if you want it to take even longer.

BACKGROUND: If you've decided to play the entire book in alphabetical order, this should make you rethink that plan. Afghanistan is possibly the simplest yet most horrible poker game ever conceived. Never charge anyone a dollar to fold. On the other hand, if you make it past this one, the rest of the book should be a picnic.

ALPHABET CITY

Seven Card Stud. The cards are ranked in alphabetical order, from highest to lowest: In other words, Aces are always high, followed by 8s, 5s, 4s, Jacks, Kings, 9s, Queens, 7s, 6s, 10s, 3s, 2s. A straight is composed of five cards out of this sequence.

BACKGROUND: Named for the Manhattan neighborhood. The deck in Alphabet City is functionally identical to a normal deck, except that Aces are always high. The only real difference is that playing this game is like trying to read a message in code. Your strategy, unless you're fluent in this code, is to bet a little, fold a lot, and play something else as soon as possible.

> Because this book contains a huge list of dealer's choice games, we thought it would be appropriate to point out a few really important ones, so that they don't get lost among the Afghanistans and Gimpsey-Doodles. The Big Ten is a list of the most popular games at our weekly poker game, which are popular either because they are solid games, because they are fun despite their weaknesses, or perhaps because we like them for no discernible reason. The first one is a unique old standard called Anaconda, a game with three rounds of card-passing, lots of players staying in, and a captivating high-low split. And that's just the basic version.

The Big Ten: ANACONDA

Each player gets seven cards. Players must now pass three cards to the left, and receive three cards from the right. Then each player passes two cards, and then one card in the same direction. Players must pass away each group of cards before looking at the next cards they will receive.

Next, players construct their best hands (this will be High-Low), and discard two cards into the center. Each player stacks the five cards in the order he wishes to reveal them, and places them in front of him, facedown. All this means that each player has seen a total of thirteen cards (a quarter of the deck) before the first bet is made, and this makes for some pretty amazing hands.

All players now roll over their top card. There is a betting round starting with the high hand. Then the next card is revealed, and so on. This process repeats until each player has only one card left facedown (obviously his most important one), at which point there is a declaration round for high, low, or both ways, followed by a showdown. (See Chapter Two for details on the procedures and rules of a declaration round.)

BACKGROUND: Named, perhaps, for the snakelike chain of cards passing around the table, Anaconda is a perennial house favorite despite some pretty serious lack of relation to real poker. One thing players love to hate about Anaconda is that they must sometimes split up a pat hand on the first pass (for example, breaking up a straight because they can only keep four cards), though the ceaseless complaining about this "problem" far overshadows the frequency of the actual problem. Plus, we think people who get pat hands should be forced to suffer.

STRATEGY: When you discard your first cards, you must decide if you're going for high or low. Sometimes it's obvious, but often it's a complete crap shoot. When everything else is equal, going for low may be the better bet. When confronted with a raw hand, a player's conditioned response is to try to improve it. There is a certain fatalistic adrenaline rush when you toss those high cards, but few pleasures equal that of seeing everyone else at the table declare for high, while you alone are going for low.

Since Aces are good for both high and low, people will almost never pass you one. If your hand requires an Ace, you're probably never going to get it. Another thing: Because you've passed so many cards, very good hands tend to win. Unless your group has a few complete amateurs or a few seasoned pros (both have their own reasons to stick around with stupid cards), you should expect a seven-player table to produce a 7- or 6-high for low and a decent full house for high nearly every time. Quads win a lot. The Wheel (5–4–3–2–A) might even split the low with another Wheel. If you're sticking around with a flush, ask yourself why.

VARIANTS: Playable with six cards, passing two, then two, then one. To break things up, assuming you're tired of passing cards to the same player all night, you can pass right, pass across, or pass dogleg left (skip a player), or any method your resident math genius can come up with. For example, in *Sidewinder*, you start by passing three to the left, then two to the *right*, and then one to the left. (In this, you can be handed your passed cards back.)

Pass the Trash: This is Anaconda without the second or third pass. Either that, or we're wrong and Anaconda is Pass the Trash without the second or third pass. Or maybe they're both the same game. Depends who you talk to. Anyway, this is a saner version of the same game because there's only one pass, so players have only laid eyes on a total of ten cards before they make their hands.

Stutter-Step Anaconda: There is no rolling step. Instead, players bet when they receive their cards, then after the first pass, then after the second and third. Then after the declaration round, hands are shown and the high and low hand split the pot (you can win both with different cards). It is also possible to play this game with a roll, meaning the game will have eight betting rounds altogether. Woo-hoo.

Avocado: Players get seven cards, then pass three to the left and three to the right at once. Then players pass two to the left and two to the right at once. Then one each way. Then play proceeds as normal for Anaconda.

Guacamole: Players get seven cards, then pass their entire hand away, four to the left and three to the right. Players make their best five-card hand and continue as above. Played only at 3 a.m., if ever.

Leeloo Dallas Multi-Pass: Pass four cards, then three, then two, then one. It's best if you slur the name of this game together, as Milla Jovovich does in her role as "Boron" in the futurist classic film *The Fifth Element*: "LEELOODALLASMULTIPASS."

Howdy Doody: Anaconda is not improved by the addition of wild cards. Nonetheless, this game exists. If a player goes for low, his Kings are wild. If a player goes for high, his 3s are wild. A player going both ways can use both wild card options for two wildly different interpretations of his magical K–K–K–K–3 hand.

Fool's Paradise: One more wild card variant. After the first pass of three cards, the dealer rolls two six-sided dice to determine the wild card's rank. (11 = Jack, 12 = Queen.) Kinda cool, because the cards atop the bell curve are typically the least useful in Anaconda, and the two best (Ace and King) aren't on the dice at all.

> ◆ **Sad but True:** The only time Mike's ever been dealt a natural straight flush was in Anaconda—right before the pass. Luckily, he passed away the low end only to be handed the high end on the last card. Okay, that part is even sadder, because it isn't true. James, on the other hand, has never been dealt a natural anything in Anaconda, and he wishes Mike would quit whining.

AUCTIONEER

Each player gets a hand of five cards. The dealer deals a face-down pile of cards into the middle of the table, containing one more card than the number of players (for example, if there are six players, the pile should have seven cards).

The dealer is the first auctioneer. The auctioneer turns over the top card of the pile, announcing out loud what it is. (Calling out the card is important so that everyone knows what the card is at exactly the same time.) Any player may now bid, out loud, any amount between 5 and 50 cents. Players may continue to outbid each other, in rapid-fire succession, until one player bids 50 cents. When a player bids 50 cents he takes the card immediately; otherwise the auction goes until the bid stops. If two players bid the same amount at the same time, the auctioneer must say "break it" and someone must make a higher bid immediately. (If two players bid 50 cents at the same time, the bid can go higher, but is usually taken by the first player to say "55.")

The card that was purchased goes into the hand of the player who bought it, and the money is paid to the pot. That player now becomes the Auctioneer, putting a card from his hand up for bids. The auctioneer calls out the card and runs the auction. A player cannot bid on a card he has just taken out of his hand.

This process continues until a card goes unbought. If no one bids on a card, it is discarded and the next card on the pile is put up for bid, with the dealer acting as auctioneer. A player may auction a card that has already been seen (changing his mind and taking it back out of his hand), as long as it is not the card he just bought. This process continues until there are no more cards in the pile and the last unbought card has been discarded. At this point all players will still have five cards.

Players now stack their cards in the order they wish to reveal them, and place the stack facedown on the table. Players reveal one card at a time and bet, starting with the high hand showing, as in Anaconda. This repeats for four rounds. After that, the fifth card is revealed and the high hand takes the pot.

VARIANTS: A shorter version of Auctioneer can be played in which there is no rolling step, just a single betting round after the auction concludes, starting with the player who bought the last card. Auctioneer can also be played High-Low, with or without a declaration phase. In this case, the second half of the game is even more like Anaconda (and the hands will be just as good). A hint: To keep your hand secret, reveal the cards you bought before the cards you started with. If you have that option.

AUCTION STUD

Seven Card Stud. Each player starts with two cards facedown. The dealer deals a row of cards equal to the number of players, faceup in the center of the table. Each player now conceals any amount of money in his hand, representing the amount he wishes to bid. When everyone is ready, all players reveal their bids. The highest bid takes first choice of the cards in the middle, adding it to his hand faceup. The next player gets the next choice, and so on. All bids are placed in the pot.

If two or more players bid the same amount, the player closest to the dealer picks first. On later rounds, this is the player closest to the left of the high hand.

After this auction, there's a betting round. Then there's another auction round followed by another betting round, and so on until all the players have seven cards. After the last betting round, there is a showdown and the high hand wins the pot.

VARIANTS: This game has much more action if played High-Low. You may also wish to cap the bidding at 50 cents, so someone can't buy the game with a series of $5 bids. But we find that in a suitably enlightened environment, the bidding tends to cap itself.

Closed Auction Stud: The seventh card for each player is dealt facedown, not auctioned. This makes your final hand look more like a normal Seven Card Stud hand.

Single-Card Auction Stud: Each round, one card is dealt in the center, and all players bid verbally for it. Players may continue to bid higher until one person buys the card; there is no maximum bid. The highest bidding player gets the card, and all other players receive a random card.

Dutch Auction Stud: Instead of dealing several cards in the center, deal them one at a time, and auction each card independently. A player who has already bought a card in one round cannot buy any more cards in that round. The player who takes the last card gets it for a nickel. This version has a lot of auctions, so you may wish to eliminate the betting rounds. That game is called, uh, *Dutch No-Bet*.

AUDITION

Five Card Stud, sort of. Each player receives three downcards and one upcard. Players must then discard two of their downcards, which are set aside in a central "talent pool." Each player now has one upcard and one downcard. Proceed from this point like Five Card Stud, with the last card faceup. Before the final betting round, the dealer shuffles the talent pool and reveals it. The lowest card among the pool is wild, as are all others of its rank. (Aces are treated as high for this purpose.)

STRATEGY: So what do you do when you get three 2s in this game? Toss one and guarantee yourself two wild cards? Keep all of them on the theory that you've got three of a kind, and might get four of something else? Don't ask us, because we've never gotten three 2s in this game. Someday we'll know.

AVIATION

Texas Hold 'Em. Each player gets a hand of four cards, and must discard one before the first bet. Each player discards a second card after the flop, and the hand continues from there as regular Hold 'Em.

BACKGROUND: Named, we think, for the seriously upscale Aviation Club de France in Paris, where they play some very French games like this one. We hope they let us in when we get rich.

BABY SEALS

Seven Card Stud. During the showdown, a player may discard one or more clubs from the seven cards in his hand. Each club so discarded can "bash" one 2, 3, or 4 (a "baby seal") in his hand, turning it into a Jack, Queen, or King (a "fur coat") of its original suit. Each of the three cards can become any of the face cards, so for example, a bashed 2 can become a Jack, Queen, or King.

BACKGROUND: Played, of course, to quietly protest the horrors of brutally savaging these foul-smelling animals for their soft, luxurious pelts.

The Big Ten: BASEBALL

> It would be strange if the game named after America's other national pastime didn't have a thousand house variants. Baseball, like the ballparks across America that bear its name, comes in a multiplicity of shapes and sizes. We'll start off with the version that seems the best, then try to give you a glimpse into the abyss of the rest.

Seven Card Stud. 3s and 9s are wild. If a player gets a 3 faceup, he must match the pot or fold. 9s are always free. If a player gets a 4 faceup, he may immediately pay a dime for an extra upcard.

BACKGROUND: Doesn't sound quite like the game you play? Get in line. As one of the most popular house games of all time, Baseball has more variations than you can imagine. No book of poker would be complete without at least one version of it, but listing all the variations would require a book by itself. One thing's certain: Baseball involves the 3s (that's the number of outs in an inning, or is it the number of strikes that puts you out?), 4s (that's the number of balls you need for a walk, or is it the number of bases?), and 9s (that's the number of innings; we're pretty sure about that one . . . unless it's the number of players in the pre-DH lineup). Strangely enough, no version seems to involve diamonds.

STRATEGY: Cards are good. Pay for every 4 you get. Pay for 3s, too, unless you're clearly beaten.

VARIANTS: In 1973, card game expert John Scarne described the following game as Baseball: Seven Card Stud, 9s are wild and faceup 4s will get you an extra card for free. Faceup 3s are death cards, i.e., catching one knocks a player out of the game. (This makes a good case for "three strikes, you're out" instead of "three outs in an inning.") In the sweetest version of Baseball we've seen, 3s and 9s are both wild and free, and so is the extra cards you get with your 4. To pick and choose from the possibilities is the dealer's prerogative, but just make sure that everybody knows what you mean when you say "Baseball."

Five Card Baseball: Five Card Stud, otherwise played as above.

Designated Hitter: Put a Joker in the deck. If a player gets the Joker facedown, it's wild, but if he gets it faceup, his hand is dead. With seven players, you technically need fifty-three cards to play Baseball (seven cards each plus a card for every 4), so adding the Joker gets you that extra card. The player you kill with that faceup Joker will be thrilled that you included that extra card to make the game more fair.

Extra Innings: The winner must have the highest heart (and, we ask, shouldn't this be the diamond?) in play to win, though it needn't be in the five cards he uses to win. Otherwise, everyone who was still in the game re-antes and the hand is redealt. This can take a long time, especially if people stick around just to show off that they have the Ace of Hearts.

Rainout: The Queen of Spades dealt faceup ends the game immediately. If so, everyone who is still alive re-antes, and the game starts over with those players.

See also Night Baseball, a game so wacky that it needs its own description and its own host of variations.

BASTARD OF SCIENCE

Five Card Draw. 2s are wild only for making pairs, 3s are wild only for making trips, 4s are wild only for making two pair and four of a kind, and 5s are wild only for straights, flushes, full houses, and straight flushes.

CLARIFICATION: The original rules we have for this game say "2s are wild for making pairs, 3s are wild for making trips, and so on." The "and so on" leaves a lot to the imagination, but the rules we've spelled out above are based on the following argument: A card is wild to complete a hand that, in essence, requires that many cards. For example, a pair is a two-card hand, three of a kind is a three-card hand, etc. A full house, which some might argue is a combination of a two- and a three-card hand, is defined in these rules as a five-card hand, so your 2s and 3s are not wild to make it.

Now, it could be argued that any poker hand is a five-card hand. But that interpretation obviously violates the spirit of this game; if you want 5s to be wild, you can just call 5s wild.

BIG SQUEEZE

Six Card Stud High-Low. After the last upcard and associated betting round, each player may pay a dollar to discard one upcard for a new upcard, or one downcard for a new downcard. There is another betting round, and the deal then continues with the final card down.

BACKGROUND: The substituted card is called a "twist." You can call pretty much any Stud game with a twist.

VARIANTS: The five-card version is called *Little Squeeze*; in this case, the twist comes after the fourth upcard.

English Stud: Big Squeeze dealt two down and four up. A twist is allowed on the third upcard, and another on the fourth upcard. To limit positional advantage, each exchange should begin with the high hand showing. English Stud doesn't normally charge for exchanges like Big Squeeze does, but of course you can if you want.

Enigma: Five Card Draw High-Low, with a twist on the last card. However, in this case a new twist option is available: A player may discard one of his upcards, turn over his hole card, and then receive another hole card. After the twist, there's a declaration round, then another betting round. (Yikes!)

BLACK AND RED

Eight Card Stud, dealt two down, five up, and one down. At the showdown, the best all-red hand splits the pot with the best all-black hand. If the deck runs out of cards on the river, the dealer must deal one faceup community card. This is possible with as few as seven players, though unlikely.

CLARIFICATION: The reason for dealing eight cards rather than seven is that on average, you'll get four cards of each color. Each player must divide his cards into two hands: one containing all his black cards, and the other all his red cards. The single best hand (red or black) opens the betting rounds, and certain hands, such as trips and quads, become impossible to make. Flushes and straights are five-card hands, so you can't claim to have a diamond flush just because your only red card is a diamond.

BACKGROUND: Known for many years as *Apartheid*. It's not often that a nickel-ante poker game is called upon to serve as an analogy for an entire sociological period in our development as rational world citizens. Even rarer is when must it bear the burden of said period being one of onerous irrationality, something that, as a people, we would wish that we could forget, but must acknowledge as something that did indeed happen, lest, as George Santayana said, "Those who forget the past are condemned to repeat it."

Yep. Not often *that* happens.

VARIANTS: Not bad as Seven Card Stud. For variety, we like to let certain cards break the color barrier.

Rosa Parks: Queens are wild and can count as either color.

The Matrix: Face cards are treated as either color. See, in the Matrix, the cool people can move back and forth between two worlds, get it? This game also has a couple of sequels. In *The Matrix Reloaded*, Aces are "The Architect"; if you have an Ace of any color, all your Queens and Kings lose their special powers, but all your Jacks become wild. And in *The Matrix Revolutions*, you use the exact same rules as *The Matrix Reloaded*; this is intended to be as disappointing as the movie.

BLACK MARIAH

Seven Card Stud. The Queen of Spades dealt faceup immediately ends the hand, and everyone who is still in the game re-antes and replays. The Queen of Spades dealt facedown splits the pot with the high hand.

BACKGROUND: The Queen of Spades gets all sorts of uncharitable names, mostly having to do with women of unsavory reputation. Despite this, Black Mariah is the most common name for this particular game, and as it turns out, a black mariah isn't a woman at all, it's a police wagon.

This game was once a whist variant involving multiple high spades. Obviously, whist players were more familiar with being forcibly hauled off to prison. This is not surprising, as whist is not the genteel game one gleans from the occasional reference in Austen or Dickens. The British held whist drives to fleece the natives from the various hellholes deemed necessary to the continuance of Her Majesty's empire. When the Nepalese Gurkhas suddenly failed to lose whatever it was they used as money, the Brits upped the ante and invented the game of bridge (or stole it from the Russians, if you believe the vodka-soaked tales). Now *that* game no one understands, least of all a poor Gurkha. Whist's dangerous cachet faded, bridge became the festival of cheating it is today, and people like us embraced the more civilized and refined poker.

BLACQUE JACQUE SHELLACQUE

Five Card Draw. The high hand splits the pot with the best Blackjack hand. A Blackjack hand, for this purpose, is a hand totaling no higher than 21, with face cards counting as 10, and Aces as the player's choice of either 1 or 11. If no hand is a legitimate Blackjack hand (most five-card hands are busts), the high hand takes the whole pot.

BACKGROUND: Named for the roughest, toughest, muk-lukest Canuck in the Klondike, against whom Bugs Bunny plays 21 in the classic Warner Brothers cartoon *Bonanza Bunny*. The wascally wabbit stands on one card, and beats Blacque Jacque's two 10s with the 21 of Hearts.

BLIND STUD

Any stud game. All cards are dealt facedown.

CLARIFICATION: You can look at your own cards. It's only called "Blind" because no one else can.

BACKGROUND: Also called *Racehorse*, for reasons lost to history. Also historically called *Mike*, for more reasons also lost to history. But Mike's not sure he wants to be associated with a game this dull. The rest of us like to call it "Mike."

BLOODLESS COUP

Seven Card Stud. All face cards are low, but are all considered the same rank. Therefore, two Queens, a King, and a Jack is a very low four of a kind.

CLARIFICATION: These low cards can't be used in straights, so the highest straight in Bloodless Coup goes to the 10.

See also Socialism *and* French Revolution for much less bloodless activity.

BLOODY SEVENS

This is a game with multiple hands, so a button denotes the "dealer" and moves to the left after each hand. Each player receives three cards facedown. Starting on the left of the button, each player must declare whether he is "in," in which case he immediately receives two more cards faceup, or "out," in which he is out of this pot but not out of the game. 7s are wild if down, but will kill a player's hand if he gets one up. "Killing" doesn't knock a player out of the game, it just guarantees that he will lose this hand.

If no one stays in but the dealer, the option passes around the table again. (Otherwise it would be too easy for the dealer to steal the pot on a round when no one else stayed in.) If not even the dealer stays in, the button moves and the hand is redealt.

After the round, the high hand takes the pot, and all losing hands (only among those players who stayed in) pay into the pot an amount equal to the size of pot. So, if 3 players go in and the pot is $1, the winner takes the pot and the two losers put $1 into the middle, growing the pot to $2. If all three of them were killed, they would all match the pot, bringing the amount on the table to $4.

Being "out" costs no money and the player is still in the game. The game ends when just one player stays in, and isn't killed. This player takes the pot.

BACKGROUND: This game barely qualifies as poker, but since it might actually involve bluffing, we decided not to embarrass it with the "games that aren't poker" header. Nonetheless, it's a game where the hammer of karma decides whether you've lived a virtuous life or whether you need to face the retribution you so richly deserve, that no earthly court can deliver, because you took the last root beer even though you *knew* we were saving it, man.

BOB DOLE

Five Card Stud. The second-best hand wins. The betting always starts with the second best hand showing.

CLARIFICATION: This seemingly innocuous little rule is really brutal, since there's really no telling what "second best hand" is going to be, and people with real monsters tend to fold at the last minute. In games such as this, one player's fold can steal the pot away from another player and hand it to a third. Because of this, we don't allow a player to fold except when he owes money to the pot.

BACKGROUND: Despite more recent available choices, we've called this game Bob Dole for so long that we should, for the sake of readers in the far future, explain who the heck Bob Dole was. Bob Dole was a U.S. senator, and rose to the position of Republican majority leader. He ran as Gerald Ford's running mate in '76, losing to Jimmy Carter, and for president in '96, losing to Bill Clinton. After leaving politics, he became a shill for Viagra. As of this writing, he is in some mysterious post-government job. Plotting.

VARIANTS: Playable with seven cards, but hoo boy. We've also seen the third-best-hand version, but can't imagine playing it.

Running Mate. The high hand splits the pot with the second-best hand. This, believe it or not, is a much more straightforward game. Name it after your favorite historical running mate, if you like. Dole's was Jack Kemp, but we're partial to Walter Mondale.

BRIAN SNŌDDY'S MIDGET PORN

Seven Card Stud. Queens are wild. Do not forget that Queens are wild. 2s and 3s are "midgets" and can be added to other number cards to create existing number cards. Thus, a 3 and a 5 can be added to make an 8, but another 3 can't be added to make an 11, because 11 isn't a real card. "A" is not a number. A combined card only has a suit if the cards that were combined to make it have the same suit (this only matters when trying to build a flush or a straight flush). Oh, and don't forget, Queens are wild.

◆ *Who's Brian Snōddy?:* Brian Snōddy (rhymes with "roadie") is an artist. We do not mean merely an illustrator, though at that he is beloved by millions. He is an artist whose medium is profanity. Swearing as an art has all but vanished. People used to have to be inventive, because if you said those seven words you can't say on TV in public, you could be *arrested*. These days, thanks to defenders of the First Amendment, God bless 'em, subtlety and innuendo are things of the past, and a few shopworn four-letter words are all you need. Brian hearkens back to an earlier time. His casual conversation is a jaw-dropping tapestry of casual profanity, delivered entirely without malice, containing only the occasional four-letter grace note, and illuminating any subject from art to science, just as long as it has midgets in it.

BACKGROUND: We love this game. We love it so much that we even have a variant, called *Clown Car.* What clown cars have to do with midgets and porn, we don't know. But we're convinced that "Brian Snōddy's Midget Porn Variant" are the five funniest words in the English language, just as "Bizarre Sausage Factory Accident" are the funniest four, "Ugandan Banana Famine" and "Removable Clown Wig" are tied for the funniest three, "Engelbert Humperdinck," though not actually English, are the funniest two, and "Pants" is the funniest one, especially when used to replace choice words in dialogue from *Star Wars*. Meanwhile, back in the poker book....

VARIANTS: *See also* Addition *and* Fusion for more fusing of cards.

Clown Car: It's the same as Midget Porn, but the best hand splits the pot with the smallest hand. "Smallest" is defined as the seven-card hand that can be compressed into the fewest cards. You have to use all seven of your cards and, yes, you can make a Queen into a midget so she can stack on top of another card. A great Clown Car hand would be something like 2–2–3–4–Q–Q–5. This can be compressed into three cards: (2 + 2 + 3 + Q)–(4 + Q)–5. And it's also four 7s: (2+5)–Q–Q–(4+3).

THE BUG

Any game. A Bug is a Joker that can be used as an Ace, or to complete a straight, flush, or straight flush. In other words, it is like a wild card, but not as wild.

BACKGROUND: Sound ridiculous? Actually, the Bug is an old idea, one you'll still find in the casino game of Pai-Gow Poker.

VARIANTS: Bugs don't have to be Jokers. You can call any game with Bugs, such as "*Locust Swarm:* 2s and 3s are Bugs," or "*System Error:* Any pair can be fused into a Bug."

CALL THE KINGS

Seven Card Stud. That's all you need to know.

BACKGROUND: Okay, here's the deal with Call the Kings. It's the only game you can call and not explain. When a King comes out faceup, everyone yells "King!" So just say you're playing Call the Kings, and don't say anything else. While the one guy who has never heard of this game is desperately going "whataretherules!?" you just casually deal the game while everyone else tells him, "Don't worry." Ideally, he will fidget and fuss and not give the dealer an ounce of trust, and the more the other players reassure him, the more he will feel like a child on his first trip to the dentist. Then, when the first King comes out and everyone yells "King" everyone should laugh, including the new guy. If the new guy doesn't laugh, ostracize him immediately.

VARIANTS: The whole point of this game is to play Seven Card Stud but act in the spirit of the wacky games your idiot friends are calling. Adding to the list of games that are basically Seven Card Stud, but with joke rules that don't really affect the game, here are a few other ways to call what sounds like a candy game and still play real poker.

Seven Nice Cards: Seven Card Stud, but players must be nice. Thank the dealer for ruining your hand, raise gently, fold with aplomb. Once you're out, you're welcome to make up for it.

Seven Angry Cards: Same as Seven Nice Cards, but you have to act angry.

Rhinoceros: All cards are wild. However, in the event of a tie, the best natural hand wins. Stunningly, the only game in this book named for a Eugene Ionesco play.

Aberrations in the Florida Voting Procedure: Named for a snippet of television news that floated through the air in a dull moment when this game was first called (feel free to use a new name each time). It's the same as Seven Card Stud, but it's called "Aberrations in the Florida Voting Procedure."

007: Seven Card Stud. If a player gets a 7 faceup, he must talk in a suave Scottish accent for the rest of the game. You haven't lived until you've heard every poker player's imitation of Sean Connery. The good ones will surprise you, the bad ones will amuse you, and everybody will give it a shot. We'd like to play this game with Sean Connery, who, after abandoning the Bond franchise to a series of struggling imitators, went on to have a four-decade career of playing himself. We expect his Sean Connery imitation is unparalleled.

CANADIAN STUD

Five Card Stud, dealt one down, three up, and one down. Two new hands are added: the four-card straight, which beats a pair, and the four-card flush, which beats a four-card straight. Both hands are lower than two pair.

BACKGROUND: Sometimes called *New York Stud* or (on a few websites) *Sökö Poker*. We don't know why, but we don't know why it'd be all that Canadian either, except for the fact that the few Canadians we know have a library of weird poker games that we've never heard of, and can't mathematically explain. For example, we once played a Canadian game where you get five cards, bet without looking, then look, and bet *again*.

CARDINAL SIN

Seven Card Stud. Kings ("Cardinals") are wild. However, if a player with a Cardinal is ever caught with a Jack in his hand, either up or down at the showdown, he is "defrocked." A player with a King and a Jack cannot win the showdown, though he may stay in the game and try to bluff everyone else out. If no one wins, everybody re-antes and says five Hail Marys, and the game is redealt to all players.

BACKGROUND: The Church. Maybe you've heard of it.

CATS AND DOGS

Five Card Stud. Four, count 'em, four new hands are introduced, all ranking between the straight and the flush. The new hands are sets of five cards of different ranks, *not including straights*, in a particular range. In descending order, they are: the big cat (any five cards from 8 to King); the little cat (any five cards from 3 to 8); the big dog (any five cards from 9 to Ace); and the little dog (any five cards from 2 to 7).

CLARIFICATION: You must have both ends of the animal in question. So a 3–4–6–7–8 is a little cat, but a 3–4–5–6–7 is a straight.

BACKGROUND: This is a very old set of hands that may haunt you repeatedly through your poker career but that will almost never show up when you play this game. They're so named because the dogs "chase" the cats. We offer this humble explanation for the rule that the dog hands are lower than the cats.

Some people believe that dogs are smarter than cats, because you can teach dogs to do tricks. Some people believe that cats are smarter than dogs for precisely the same reason. To break this tie, it's important to imagine each animal in the opposite situation. If you can teach a cat to do tricks, you will have little trouble finding someone who will say, "That is one smart cat." However, if you have a dog that cannot learn any tricks, you will have a harder time finding anyone to declare, "That is one smart dog."

Intelligence notwithstanding, cats turn out to be better pets because they outrank dogs on most other tests, including ductility, tensile strength, conductivity, and specific gravity. They only score poorly on the sympathy and hardness tests, which are essentially the same test, involving dropping the animals from a great height onto a nail.

CENTIPEDE

Seven Card Stud. Each table position is assigned a different wild card. For the player to the immediate left of the dealer, 2s are wild. For the next player, 3s are wild, and so on. Each player's wild cards are the same for the whole game; they are not reassigned when someone folds.

BACKGROUND: Named for the segmented arthropod, though we never quite get up to making 100s wild.

CHALLENGE

This is a multi-round game, so you must use a button that represents the dealer. Each player antes a nickel and receives a hand of two cards. Starting on the left of the button, each player in turn must declare whether he is "in" or "out," until one player calls that he is "in." Proceeding from there, and including all players who have already gone "out," each player in turn can decide whether or not to "challenge" the player who is in. Each of these players will show down in secret against the "in" player, by exchanging their cards facedown, and in each case the loser of the two hands pays the winner the amount in the pot. If no one challenges the "in" player, the game ends and that player takes the pot. If no one goes "in," no money is exchanged and the game continues.

After the two-card round, players ante another nickel and receive three more cards, giving them a hand of five. Repeat the challenge step, as above. Then ante again and play with seven cards. After the seven-card round, move the button one player to the left, shuffle, and repeat. This continues until one player goes unchallenged, at which point the game ends and that player takes the pot.

CLARIFICATION: Here's an example. The cards are dealt, and Agnes and Bill pass. Chuck goes in. Three players, including Darryl, Enid, and Agnes, go in against Chuck. He shows his hand in secret to each of these challengers, looking at each of their hands in turn. He wins one of the challenges and loses two. He pays the amount in the pot to the two players who beat him, and collects that amount from the one player he beat. On the second round, Enid goes in, but no one challenges her. Enid wins the game and takes the pot.

VARIANTS: *See* 3–5–7 for a much nastier version of this game, with wild cards, legs, and multi-hand showdowns.

CHERNOBYL

There are two versions of Chernobyl, White and Black.

White Chernobyl: Seven Card Stud. Treat all face cards as 10s. (So a Jack and a 10 is a pair of 10s.) Any player who receives two pair or better faceup is immediately declared the winner. Because of positional advantage, the dealer starts each dealing round after the first with the high hand, rather than the hand on the dealer's left.

Black Chernobyl: Seven Card Stud. Treat all face cards as 10s. Any player who receives two pair (or better) faceup is immediately out of the game. Deal to the high hand first. In addition, players may pay 50 cents to "suppress" their fourth upcard, and receive it facedown. The dealer must ask each player whether he wants to do this immediately before dealing that player his card.

BACKGROUND: The city of Chernobyl has provided us with many things, including Maria Sharapova, two fine poker variants, a nearly limitless supply of thyroid cancer, and a moving episode of Michael Palin's *Pole to Pole*.

VARIANTS: We're not out of nuclear tragedies yet, pal.

Three Mile Island: Anyone who gets three of a kind or better is either the winner (in White) or knocked out (in Black). Same game, but ever so slightly more stable.

The Big Ten: CHICAGO

◆ Any game that figures prominently in *Rounders* probably ought to be in our top ten. Okay, so they only played it once. But they used it because it's a great example of a game that's easy to cheat at: One card (the Ace of Spades) guarantees you half the pot. It's a boring game when one card is a guaranteed win, and Chicago only really gets interesting once the Ace and King are faceup. But it's still fun if, you know, no one cheats.

Seven Card Stud. The high hand splits the pot with the highest spade in the hole. The Ace of Spades is the highest spade, and guarantees half the pot to anyone who holds it facedown. If no one has a spade down, the high hand takes the whole pot.

BACKGROUND: On a trip to Chicago in 2004, James had the unique experience of teaching this game to a bunch of card players who had never heard of it. You would think that someone in a group of eight poker players in the heart of Chicago would have heard of the game, since it's called Chicago, but no. The funniest thing was that they immediately decided it was the best game ever. Okay, no, the even funnier thing was that they kept forgetting what it was called.

Regardless, this traditional game ostensibly came from Chicago, though when it left town, it must not have left a note. There's no particular reason we can think of that explains the name of the game. Or its popularity, for that matter. Despite simple rules, Chicago is a candy game of the most obnoxious stripe, because a player can know from the beginning that he's getting half the pot. It's nice to be able to raise the heck out of the pot once you get a lock on half of it, but it's no fun for the rest of us, who are battling like titans for the legitimate half of the prize.

STRATEGY: Get a high spade. It's a little strange that a high card is the key card. This means that if you have an Ace, King, or Queen of Spades down you're in a good position to get the best hand as well as the high spade. That explains why "Low Chicago" is the most commonly played variant, since at least in that game the card that cinches half the pot isn't that great for winning the other.

VARIANTS: The other three suits have their own versions of this game, sometimes called *Philadelphia* (hearts), *Detroit* (clubs), and *Beverly Hills* (diamonds). All three games can be altered by any of the following variations. We'll let you come up with all the clever names for the ones we haven't listed.

Chicago Suburbs: The high hand splits the pot with the player who has the most spades in the hole. If there is a tie for most spades, the one with the higher spade takes it. For example, if the down spades are A♠, 10♠–3♠ and K♠–Q♠, the player with the K♠–Q♠ takes half the pot.

Cold Hands, Warm Heart: Same rules as High Chicago but the high heart, not the high spade, splits the pot, and one player *can't take both.* The player with the best hand is disqualified from holding the high heart, and the split therefore goes to the second highest heart. This is interesting because at least it keeps the player with the lock on half the pot from getting lucky and taking the other half too!

Low Chicago: Same as High Chicago, but the low spade splits the pot with the best hand. For this purpose, Aces are always high, so the best spade to have is the Deuce.

Low Chicago Lowball: The low hand (see Lowball) splits the pot with the low spade in the hole. Again, the Deuce is the lowest spade for purposes of pot splitting.

Low Chicago Low Hole Wild: The lowest card in a player's hole is wild, as are others of that rank, and the low down spade splits the pot with the best hand. Again, the low spade (and the lowest hole card) is the deuce, not the Ace. As in Low Hole Wild (see that), a player can pay 50 cents to get his last card faceup.

Bob Hope Celebrity Golf Classic: The high hand splits the pot with the player holding the fewest clubs. For your fewest-clubs hand, you must play all seven cards.

Blow Chicago: The high hand splits the pot with the highest hole card. If there's a tie for highest hole card, the high hand gets the whole pot. That Ace seems less of a sure thing than one might expect.

CINCINNATI

Each player gets a hand of five cards, and another hand of five cards is dealt facedown in the center. The dealer deals these cards like a normal hand; i.e., one card after each player gets their first card, one after each gets their second, and so on. The central cards are community cards, and can be used in any player's hand.

Turn over the first community card and have a round of betting. Expose the second card, have another bet, and so on for all five cards. In the showdown, a player may use any combination of the five cards in his hand and the five cards on the table.

BACKGROUND: Cincinnatians vent their frustrations by doing bizarre things to chili, and apparently, no one can stop them. We've never understood that, nor why they would associate themselves with a game also dubbed *Lame Brain*. The community cards just might be the best five card hand on the table, and then *everybody wins*. Okay, this is only going to happen once in every hundred thousand hands, but the possibility is inescapably obvious.

VARIANTS: Cincinnati can be played High-Low, but you can pretty much expect everyone to stay in until the end. That's okay. You came here to gamble, right?

Cincinnati Liz: The last center card revealed and all of that rank are wild.

Lame Brain Pete: The lowest card in the center and all of that rank are wild. (Cincinnati itself is sometimes called Lame Brain Pete. At our house, we reserve this name for the low-card-wild variant.)

Tennessee: This is the same as Cincinnati, except the betting structure is different. When the first community card is exposed, the opening bet (if there is any) must be a nickel, and all raises must be a dime. When the second center card is exposed, opening costs a dime, and raising 20 cents. The subsequent cards are 15 cents to open and 30 to raise, 20 to open and 40 to raise, and 25 to open and 50 to raise.

CONTROL

Seven Card Stud. After the fourth upcard is dealt, the person with the best hand showing (the "controller") decides whether the game will continue or be redealt. If he opts to continue, the hand proceeds as normal. If not, the game is redealt and everyone who has not folded re-antes and plays again.

VARIANTS: This game is kind of stupid, frankly. It's a good 2 a.m. game when you're trying to convince everyone it's time to go home. For a low-impact version, allow the controller to determine something more trivial, such as what game to play next, who pays for the beer, who should be President of the United States, etc.

KAOS: The role of controller is determined by the rank of the fourth upcard, not by who has the best hand. Break ties in rank by using suit order (highest suit is spades, then hearts, diamonds, and clubs). Ha! You thought the other game went on forever.

Two-Thirds: To win, you must hold two of three possible winning hands. The winning hands are the highest ranking hand, the highest spade in the hole, and the lowest spade in the hole. After the fourth upcard is dealt, the person with the best hand showing has control as above. If no one person has two of the three winning hands at the showdown, you re-ante and redeal.

COUNCIL BLUFFS

Also known as *Omaha-"X."* It is Omaha-8, which is Omaha with a high-low split requiring an 8 or better to qualify for low, except that the rank of the qualifier is determined by the river card. For example, if the board is 5–6–J–K–10, then a 10-high will qualify for low. If the river is a 4 or lower (including Ace), there is no possible low hand, since you can't have an unpaired hand the highest card of which is a 4, and if the river is a King then any unpaired hand can qualify for low.

BACKGROUND: Omaha is a city of empty superlatives. A tour of the city with an enthusiastic resident will reveal a number of local claims to fame including the world's largest geodesic dome, world's largest pot of coffee, Nebraska's longest continuous concrete pour, and plans for the world's longest pedestrian bridge. Unfortunately, they're *not* host to the world's largest game of Omaha, because as of this writing, there are no casinos in Omaha. This is due primarily to the strong anti-gambling lobby backed almost entirely by the casinos across the river in Council Bluffs, Iowa. That pedestrian bridge will come in handy if they ever build it, at least for any Omaha residents who actually want to play Omaha. It probably won't surprise you to hear, but you pretty much can't play Hold 'Em in Texas, either.

COUNTDOWN

Seven Card Stud. The rank of the wild card always equals the number of live players.

CLARIFICATION: For example, if there are four live players, 4s are wild. If there are three players in the showdown (which is the only time the wild card really matters), 3s are wild. As with other games where one player's fold can ruin someone else's hand, the only legal time to fold is when the action is on you, and you can only fold in Countdown when you owe money to the pot. You can't suddenly fold for free or in the middle of the showdown.

Best Countdown game ever: In one recent game, the upcards Mike dealt were two Aces, three 2s, and three 3s. Really! You can't make up stuff like that!

BACKGROUND: The obligatory joke is, "If everyone else folds, are my Aces wild?" Every time you explain this game, someone will ask that question. You can set your watch by it. Try answering, "If everyone else folds, the last player is forced to take the pot and must stop betting. He may, however, continue to ask stupid questions."

STRATEGY: Countdown rewards you for betting the max early and often. Basically, you want to get enough people to fold that your 3 of Hearts becomes useful. The easiest way is to bet like a drunken sailor and hope that everyone else folds in disgust. Sadly, everyone else is wise to your little game, and they also have low cards, so what you actually get is a game of chicken, where everyone bets and raises enormous sums on hands that are only *potentially* good. Few things are as hilarious as a game where everyone has stuck it out to the bitter end, and the losers have to justify to themselves why they stayed in with a pair of Treys and an Ace.

VARIANTS: Sometimes we improve a poker game by adding a match-the-pot rule. This isn't one of those times.

How Stupid Are You?: When a player receives a wild card face-up, he must either match the pot or fold. Note that matching the pot in this game is dramatically stupid, since your card isn't likely to be wild by the end. On the plus side, this game does reduce the percentage of smart players in the showdown.

COURCHEVEL

Omaha. The flop is exposed prior to the first bet.

BACKGROUND: Named for the tony French ski resort, intimating that European gentlemen wouldn't deign to bet before knowing seven-ninths of their cards.

VARIANTS: Sometimes played as *Omaha-8.* The number

of the board cards can also vary quite a bit. We've heard of this game using a two-card flop, then one, then one, for a total of four community cards; or two, then two, then one, for a total of five; or one, then two, for a total of three community cards (of which you would have to use all three). The one flop pattern that makes the most sense to us, despite the fact that we've never heard of it, is to reveal the cards 1-3-1, since that gives players less information on which to base their initial bet.

CRYOGENIC FREEZE

Seven Card Stud, with the last five cards dealt faceup. The last card dealt to a player is wild, as are all others like it in his hand. After each betting round, but before the deal, a player may "freeze" his hand. This means he's still in the game, but he will get no more cards (and therefore the last card he received will remain wild). Use a marker or some method of denoting that your hand is frozen, so the dealer doesn't accidentally deal to you. Once frozen, a hand can never get more cards.

BACKGROUND: The game is based on an old science-fiction idea. Someday, when you get an incurable disease, instead of dying, they'll freeze you and you'll sleep for hundreds of years until they can revive you in a future free from disease or death, where, as a primitive with no grasp of modern science, language, or mores, you'll toil in the radium mines of Mercury. Or hit .406 for the BoSox. Your call, really.

CLARIFICATION: Players must still bet to stay in this game (unlike in Demolition Man, below) even when they stop receiving cards. Straights and flushes are five-card hands, so if a player has fewer than five cards, he can't make these hands.

DEMOLITION MAN

Eight Card Stud High-Low, dealt two down, five up, and one down. Jacks ("Simon Phoenix") are "poison," and Kings ("John Spartan") are "heat." If a Jack is dealt faceup, all upcards that are not frozen (see below) must be discarded. If a King is dealt faceup, all frozen hands are unfrozen. After each betting round, a player may "freeze" his hand, meaning that he will receive no more cards and no longer has to bet, unless his hand is unfrozen. Mark the frozen hands to show that they are immune to poison and do not get cards.

The pot is split between best high and best low hands, but to qualify for low you must have at least five cards.

CLARIFICATION: Players do not have to bet when they are frozen (unlike in Cryogenic Freeze). Straights and flushes are five-card hands, so if a player has less than five cards, he can't make these hands. And you also need five cards to qualify for low.

BACKGROUND: This game is, as the name would suggest, a cross between Nemesis and Cryogenic Freeze. But with Wesley Snipes.

When *Demolition Man* came out, one of the most outlandish jokes in the film, along with the notion that all restaurants had become Taco Bell and that Denis Leary was in charge of anything, was that Arnold Schwarzenegger had been elected President thanks to his popularity and a constitutional amendment that allowed him to run. Like all good science-fiction (including *The Running Man*, itself a Schwarzenegger film in which a barrage of sadistic reality shows distracts the American public from the outrageous excesses of a corrupt regime and a man buys plane tickets on the internet), this film gets less unrealistic every day.

The Big Ten: DIABLO

> Diablo has been a staple at Phil's poker nights forever, but we can't find any game like it listed anywhere else. Not even a weird version by another name. We've decided to list it in our Big Ten because it's time the world learned to love to hate this game as much as we do. Diablo is a fascinating and wonderful pot-matching game that rewards guts with glory, caution with regret, and stupidity with soul-crushing justice.

Five Card Draw, Deuces wild. There is a maximum draw of two cards. If you open, you must win; if the opener doesn't win, the winner takes the pot but the opener must replace it. If no one opens, everyone throws their hand in, re-antes, and the game is dealt again. There will be multiple rounds, so use a button to designate the dealer, and move the button to the left after each deal. If you fold, you are out of the game for good. The game ends when the opener actually wins. This can easily happen on the first round, but that's no fun, so we usually play again.

CLARIFICATION: The "opener" is the first player to make a bet, just as in any other game. It's an important designation in this game, however, because the opener is obligated to win, or replace the pot. When the hand is redealt, players only re-ante if there was no opener. If the hand is actually played, there is no ante on the next deal, because the loser has "anted for everyone." The second betting round starts on the left of the button, regardless of bets, just as it does in normal Five Card Draw.

BACKGROUND: This most evil of games spread from Phil's house like a pox. We've now seen it at dozens of conventions. It later spawned a monstrosity called Frankenstein, the other game of this stripe that almost made our Big Ten. Open that Pandora's box at your own risk.

STRATEGY: Table position is critical in this game, since you can open with far worse cards when you act last. What "good cards" means is a little iffy, but we suggest you don't open without at least three of a kind. (When the opener draws two cards, it's traditional to chant, "Trips! He opened on trips!") If you hold Deuces, your hand is much better than if you don't, since wild cards in other players' hands can be deadly to you. Don't open the pot with a drawing hand (i.e., four to a flush) unless (a) you have a wild card and therefore more chances of catching something, (b) you act late in the round and are probably up against inferior hands, and (c) you are crazy. A drawing hand is much better for calling than opening, so keep your fingers crossed and hope someone else opens.

A player who opens and then stands pat is likely sitting on a straight or flush. If you believe this, your best bet is to try to draw to a full house or better, if you have a choice. He might still beat you with quads, but at least you did the best you could. A pat straight, nice though it may look, is a risky hand to open with since it won't be improved on the draw.

After the draw, try to get a sense of whether the opener will win by watching who else is betting. Even if you will certainly lose this hand, as long as the opener doesn't win, the pot

will still be there on the next hand. This means you'll be competing for the same pot next time with, possibly, a smaller pool of opponents.

VARIANTS: Enough nickel antes and quarter bets can grow this pot to double-digit dollars before you know it. If your entire group is averse to matching a pot that big, the game may degenerate into hand after hand of everyone throwing their cards away until someone starts with quads. Once a player does open, the pot odds are so good you'd be a fool to throw your hand away, which will grow the pot even more. You can reduce the stress on the opener by capping his penalty at $5. Let the pot grow as big as it wants, but when the opener loses, make him pay no more than $5 back into the pot. Or, if you're playing normally and the pot gets out of control, players can agree to split whatever's there after a fixed number of deals.

DIAMONDS AREN'T FOREVER

Seven Card Stud. If a player is dealt a faceup diamond and bets (that is, doesn't check) when it's his action in that round, he may kill that diamond upcard by pitching it faceup into the center. All other cards of that rank are also dead, and are immediately pitched into the center. If a dead card is facedown, hold on to it; it's still dead, but at least it's a secret. If no one has any live cards by the showdown, all surviving players re-ante and the game is redealt.

CLARIFICATION: You only get one shot per diamond, and only if you pay money to the pot first. Even if a diamond is your top upcard, you can only use it as a kill card if you got it this round.

BACKGROUND: An excellent game if your hand bites and you want to spread some of the misery around. To get in the proper mind-frame, pretend you're North Korea, and you've got missiles. This will distract you from the fact that it doesn't actually make sense to call this game Diamonds Aren't Forever, since they disappear but destroy the other suits when they go. Maybe it ought to be called *Live and Let Diamond*. Or *Diamond Another Day*. Or *A View to a Kill . . . Of Diamonds!*

DOUBLE-BARREL DRAW

Five Card Draw. This game is dealt as Jacks or Better (Five Card Draw, with a pair of Jacks or better required to open), and continues to the showdown as such if anyone opens the pot. However, if no one opens, the game becomes straight Lowball and the initial bet goes around again, this time with no opening requirement.

BACKGROUND: In his 1949 book *Scarne on Cards*, John Scarne calls this game Lowball. In his 1973 *Encyclopedia of Games* he reverses himself, and calls this game Double-Barrel Draw while also listing the modern version of Lowball. It would seem that the definition of Lowball changed between those two books, or that one book was in error. But in both books Scarne describes this game as exceptional, and we agree with him. By any name, this is a game worth playing. Maybe even all the time.

DOUBLE DOWN

Five Card Stud (maximum of five players). Each player gets two downcards, which become the first cards of two separate hands. Each player is then dealt two upcards, and must assign one upcard to each of those hands. Then a betting round occurs, starting with the single highest hand. Before the next three betting rounds, each player gets two upcards and must assign each card to one of to the two hands. Once a card is assigned, it can't be moved. If a player folds, he must fold both hands. At the showdown, the highest hand wins the pot.

BACKGROUND: This game is for those people who want the maximum amount of poker experience in the smallest amount of time, usually before they're sent back into solitary. This, alas, is yet another symptom of our ever-accelerating world. Back in the '40s, the official rules of poker said if a player called time, he had a maximum of five minutes to make his bet. If everyone did that, a single hand could take two hours. No time for nonsense like that now. Let's play two.

VARIANTS: Playing High-Low is good. All these games max out at five players.

Henway: All players get ten cards to start. They must split them into two five card hands and then roll them one at a time (actually, two at a time), betting between each roll. The highest hand wins (this can also be High-Low). Named for the joke with the punchline "About five pounds," for no reason we can discern.

Ten Card Regrets: Five Card Stud High-Low. Each player receives ten cards facedown and does not look at them. Before each round of betting, each player draws two cards from his stack and places one faceup to each side of his stack. The left stack is played for low, and the right stack is played for high. Cards cannot be switched after being placed. If a player folds, he must fold both hands. At the showdown, compare all live low hands, then all live high hands. (To make bluffing possible, each player can roll two cards as normal on the first turn, draw his next two cards and *then* bet. Then those cards are laid down, and then two more cards are drawn before the next bet. This cuts the betting rounds to four, with players having two cards in hand until the showdown.)

Always a Bridesmaid: Using the same rules as Double Down

or Henway, your choice, the high hand splits the pot with the second-best hand. (Look under Bob Dole for other games featuring the second best hand.)

DOUBLE DRAW

Five Card Draw, with a maximum of five players or six if you add two Jokers. Players bet on their starting hands, then discard up to two cards and draw replacements, then bet, then discard and draw up to two more, and bet again.

BACKGROUND: This is a good game if you believe Five Card Draw has too few betting rounds, which we would agree with. The hands are usually a lot better than in Five Card Draw.

VARIANTS: If you have more than five players, you can draw two cards then one, or even one then one.

Triple Draw: This has three drawing rounds of one card each, and can be played by as many as six players, even without Jokers. You can also play Triple Draw drawing 2–1–1, which takes the required number of cards back up to nine per player.

Discord: Either Double Draw or Triple Draw, with this rule: Each time, after everyone has discarded cards, all discards are turned faceup before the bet. "Discards" includes the cards that were thrown away and drawn for, but not folded hands. Discards are kept in front of the player rather than tossed in the center like folded hands. We like this game because it improves upon Five Card Draw with extra betting, and some arbitrary but seemingly useful knowledge about other players' hands.

DOWNTOWN

Seven Card Stud. If a player's upcards aren't dealt in rank order, either from lowest to highest or highest to lowest, his hand is dead. Before dealing the third and fourth upcards, the dealer must ask each player if he wishes to skip this deal. That player receives no card, but is still in the game. A player can't change the order of his upcards.

CLARIFICATION: If you skip one deal, you can still get cards on the next. Neighboring cards of the same rank don't disturb the sequence, so 3–5–5–9 (or 9–5–5–3) doesn't kill the hand. You first two cards can't possibly be out of order, but if they are a King and a Deuce, you'll probably want to quit taking cards. Aces can be high or low, so if your first upcard is an Ace, only your fourth upcard can kill you. If your first two upcards are Aces, you've got it made. But then, you probably already knew that.

BACKGROUND: These streets go one way. Any sufficiently urbanized area decides at some point to make all its streets one-way, as if somehow this lets them put the same amount of city in half the space.

See also Uptown for a nice thematic complement. If you're into that sort of thing.

DO YA?

Five Card Stud, hole card wild. Each player starts with a down-card, which is wild for that player (along with others of its rank). Starting on the left of the dealer, each player is dealt one upcard. The player may take his first card or decline it, in which case a second upcard is dealt. Again he may take or decline it, in which case he is dealt a third upcard which he must take.

The next player may choose from any card left over from the previous player's cards, or he may decline and get a new choice. If there is only one leftover card, he can refuse a second card and be forced to take a third. Once a player gets a third card, he must take it. This process continues until everyone has one upcard. The left-over upcards are discarded, and there is a betting round.

This process happens three more times, each subsequent deal beginning with the high hand, until everyone has five cards. A final betting round occurs, and the best hand takes the pot.

BACKGROUND: Apparently, this is the real Do Ya? We had this confused with The Price is Right. Thanks to the wonders of the e-interweb, we've been set straight.

VARIANTS: This can also be played High-Low, or straight Lowball. The low version of Do Ya? is called *Yoo Da*. Or *Yoda*, if you're among the generation who find *Star Wars* amusing.

DR. PEPPER

Seven Card Stud. 2s, 4s, and 10s are wild.

BACKGROUND: Get this. Back in the day, a study on fatigue showed that people's energy dropped to its lowest points at 10:30, 2:30, and 4:30. So the makers of Dr. Pepper put a mysterious "10–2–4" emblem on their bottle, reminding people to drink three energy-rich servings of prune-flavored caffeine at those critical hours of the day, presumably in addition to the Dr. Peppers they were already drinking at breakfast, lunch, and dinner. Now, unless you're Forrest Gump, drinking this much Dr. Pepper will probably kill you. But kudos for the marketing genii at Dr. Pepper, whose sales pitch resulted not only in a poker game with twelve, count 'em, twelve wild cards, but also a generation of jittery, insomniac poker players for whom eleven wild cards would never have been enough.

DUCK KONUNDRUM

Seven Card Stud, requiring a hat, scrap paper, and a live duck. Before the game begins, each player writes down a rule that could apply to a Seven Card Stud game, such as "Lowball" or "Deuces wild," or even a collection of rules that are already known by one name, such as "Hamlet." The rule can't change the number of betting rounds or the concept that the ranking of poker hands determines the winning player, but can otherwise be pretty much anything. The rules are written on slips of scrap paper, which are folded and placed into the hat.

Before each betting round, the duck draws a rule from the hat and, to the best of his ability, reads it aloud. That rule applies for the rest of the game. If a rule contradicts a previous rule, the second rule takes precedence in the simplest and least destructive way possible. (For example, "Jacks are the highest card" is drawn, followed by "4s are the highest card." 4s are now higher than Jacks, which are still higher than Aces.) Rules can't affect cards simultaneously if they are contradictory; for example, a card can't be both wild and dead. (While some games cover this specific case, there are too many possibilities here to be covered by a general rule).

CLARIFICATION: If you do not have a duck, a reasonable substitute may be used, but with a far less satisfying result.

BACKGROUND: Named for a popular activity at the Massachusetts Institute of Technology, invented by student Dan Katz (note the initials). Quack!

VARIANTS: The fact that you reading the sentence after the word "Variants" after the game described above disqualifies you from learning any variant rules that might exist. May you be cursed with the duck that cannot read.

EIGHT OR BETTER

Seven Card Stud High-Low. You need an 8 or better to qualify for low, which means that a five-card hand that is competing for "low" can't have a card higher than 8. Straights and flushes do not count against you for low, so the wheel (A–2–3–4–5) is the best low hand. There is no declaration round, and a player can win high and low with the same five cards or with a different set. If there's no qualifying low, the high hand wins the whole pot.

BACKGROUND: Also called *Seven-Eight*, this is one of the finest ways to play a High-Low split pot game. Most casino poker rooms play Omaha-8, a High-Low split game with the same requirement of an 8 or better for low. The fact that you must actually qualify for low makes a player more willing to fold rather than stay in with any seven cards, hoping to simply be the worst hand among all the players who stayed in.

FEATHERS MCGRAW

Seven Card Stud. The player with the high hand showing is the "penguin." The betting rounds always start to the left of the penguin. During the second and subsequent betting rounds, on his action, a player may accuse the penguin of being the "chicken." Those two players secretly compare downcards. If the accuser has a higher hand, the penguin puts his fingers straight-up atop his head and folds his hand, and a new penguin is declared. If the penguin has a higher hand, the accuser must fold and pay the pot to the penguin. On later rounds, the high hand may change, and with it the identity of the penguin. If there's one live player left, he gets the pot; otherwise, the winner of the showdown does.

BACKGROUND: This game is based on Nick Park's Wallace and Gromit short *The Wrong Trousers*. In it, Feathers McGraw is a harmless-looking-yet-sinister penguin who commits crimes while disguised as a harmless-looking-yet-sinister chicken (that is, with a highly effective rubber glove stuck on his head). When he removes the glove, everyone (that is, everyone but the audience) is stunned at the abject duplicity of it all.

FIVE AND DIME

Seven Card Stud. 5s and 10s are wild. If a player gets a 5 face-up, he must mark it with a quarter to keep it wild. The same is true with 10s, but for 50 cents. The coins on the cards are part of the pot; they just serve as reminders that the wild cards were paid for. If a player doesn't pay for a faceup 5 or 10, it isn't wild. Facedown 5s and 10s are always wild.

BACKGROUND: Back when there were stores called "five and dimes" and this game could actually be called *Woolworth* and make sense, 5s cost a nickel and 10s cost a dime. But nowadays, in a nickel-ante game, that's so cheap it's like free. Even at 25 and 50 cents, this game is still much tamer than its wicked half-brother, Heinz 57.

VARIANTS: When you're in a good mood, the 5s and 10s can be free. When you're in a bad mood, the cost for not paying for a wild card can be folding, in which case there's no need to mark the cards with coins. If they're up, they must have been paid for.

The Big Ten: FOLLOW THE QUEEN

◆ That Queen sure gets around. Follow the Queen may be the most popular game in the world of nickel poker. It's got so many variants that we still have to declare which rules we're using, even though we wrote the book. "Follow the Queen," the dealer will say. "Are Queens wild?" asks the chorus. "Of course," he replies, or "Of course not," depending on who he is and what mood he's in. "And if the last card dealt up is a Queen?" they will chant. And so the dance continues.

Seven Card Stud. When a Queen is dealt faceup, the next card is wild, as are others like it. When another Queen is dealt faceup, it cancels the first wild card and creates a new one. If the last card dealt faceup is a Queen, nothing is wild.

CLARIFICATION: Notice that we didn't say, "Queens are wild." We don't play that way, but your friends might, so whenever you call this game, be sure to specify. That's a bad rule to get wrong.

BACKGROUND: Why do most games that single out a face card choose the Queen to be the card of note? The exceptions tend to pick on the afflicted, such as the one-eyed Jacks. Is it because the Queens look so bored? Fair's fair, the Kings and the Jacks don't look like they're having fun either; one King has even taken the easy way out. But the guys are more posed, more formal. They've got a job to do and they're going to do it, whereas the Queens just stand around holding those stupid flowers. They should at least get something to occupy their time, and that's what this classic game gives them.

STRATEGY: When you have a temporary wild card, you must bet aggressively, assuming you have any hope of forcing players out. If players leave, fewer upcards are dealt, which reduces the chances of another Queen coming up and wrecking your wild card. Of course, if you can count all the Queens, you don't have to worry so much. But if you have a permanent wild card, bet even more!

VARIANTS: Some variants are obvious: Follow the Jack, Follow the King, and so on. You can also play as Five or Six Card Stud. The games below use the same rules, with more interesting exceptions. In most, you still must decide whether Queens are wild.

Follow Mariah: The other three Queens act normally, but the Queen of Spades causes the hand to be redealt. (See Black Mariah for details.)

Graphite Fire: Once a card is wild, it remains wild. Don't make Queens wild unless you want, what, something like twenty wild cards.

Heisenberg: Instead of becoming wild, the upcard after the Queen determines the rules for the game: If that card is low, i.e., 2 through 7, the game becomes Lowball. If it's high, or if the last upcard is a Queen, then the high hand wins.

Lie Still and Think of England: The upcard dealt on top of a Queen becomes wild, not the next card dealt in sequence. Don't play with Queens wild, since a Queen would give one player two wild cards. After all, you didn't sign up for anything "wacky."

Precede the Jack: If a Jack comes up, the card dealt just before it is wild. This means the last player's last card can't possibly be wild, since it can't precede a Jack. (If the dealer complains about getting fewer wilds because of his table position, he should call a different game.) Jacks are usually wild in this variant, since dealers are usually looking out for number one.

Rich Bitch: When you get any wild card faceup you must pay a quarter or fold.

Touch of Evil: The card after the Queen isn't wild, it's dead. The same game with Jacks is called *Jack Cheese*, while the one with Kings is called *King Rat*.

Typhoid Mary: The card after the Queen isn't wild. Instead, the card the Queen lands on (i.e., the previous upcard dealt to the same player) becomes dead, along with others like it. Once dead, cards are permanently dead even if new Queens are dealt.

Yellow Brick Road ("Follow the Follow the Follow the Queen"): Queens start wild. When a card follows a Queen, Queens stop being wild and the new card becomes wild. When a second copy of the new card is dealt, it stops being wild and the third card becomes wild, and so on. This sounds like it will get crazy, but it usually results in only one or two switches.

Rosencrantz and Guildenstern: This game is "Follow the Hamlet," and is so complicated that it gets its own listing. Let that be a warning to you.

So What If the Last Faceup Card Is a Queen?: For some reason, the positional advantage in Follow the Queen rankles some players, despite the fact that many other games have it much worse (No-Peekum, Heinz 57, and even Five Card Draw come to mind). The argument goes like this: The player in the first position receives one card that can never follow a Queen (i.e., his first upcard), so he's "cheated" out of a potential wild. One hare-brained solution is an extra rule saying that we remember the first card, even if that player folds, and if the last upcard is a Queen, that first card is wild. We would argue that the first player already has enough advantage, because he's the player who, on subsequent rounds, can know he's getting a wild card before he even has to bet, if the last card dealt on the previous round was a Queen. Giving this guy one extra little bonus is like buttering a cake. A better solution would be to burn a card before dealing, and if that card is a Queen, the first player's card is wild. But this seat really has it pretty good already. If anything, for fairness, other players should be allowed to kick him under the table every time he speaks.

FRANKENSTEIN

Five Card Draw with a "Monster hand." A button signifies the dealer, and moves to the left after each hand. The button deals Five Card Draw as normal, limiting the draw to two cards if there are seven or more players, and to three once the number of players is below six. Discarded cards (this does not include the folded hands) are gathered in the center and create a Monster hand. At the showdown, the player with the best hand must beat the Monster. If he doesn't, he must match the pot, and a new hand is dealt. If a player folds, he is out of the game for good.

CLARIFICATION: The only legal time to fold is when the action is on you. In Frankenstein, you can fold at this point even when you do not owe money to the pot, since by having the highest hand you may be forced to pay more money if you stay in.

BACKGROUND: Based loosely on the novel by Mary Shelley. Don't embarrass yourselves, kids; Frankenstein is the scientist, not the monster.

STRATEGY: As long as there are several players in the game, your safest bet is to discard very good cards and try not to be the player who is brutalized by the Monster. Because of this tactic, the game tends to resemble Lowball for the first few hands, with high hands folding in terror, until it gets to the point where someone thinks he can go for the high hand and actually win. This tipping point will vary depending on your table position and what other players are doing.

Because it's the high hand that gets hurt, you may find yourself inclined to fold if you draw a decent hand (two pair, for example) that probably can't beat the Monster. But it's also possible to stick around with medium-strength hands, grit your teeth through the pot matching, and come back to win back all your money plus a little more.

Oh, and if you have a pat low and you want to hurt someone, bet a lot. Follow your announcement of the size of your bet with the words "of pain."

FRENCH REVOLUTION

Seven Card Stud. A player may use any 2, 3, or 4 in his hand (a "Peasant") to kill one of his face cards (an "Aristocrat"), simultaneously making the Peasant wild. This decision is made at the showdown. It takes a dead Aristocrat to make a Peasant wild, so if you have no face cards, you can't have any wild cards.

BACKGROUND: France is a wonderful place. The food is terrific, and the people are wonderfully helpful and polite (as soon as they realize that you're not German). They also demonstrated a method of cultivating a ruling elite who ground the other 98% of the population under their heels, then slaughtering them like the swine they were. We can learn many things from France.

VARIANTS: Some players prefer face cards to be automatically dead, but those cards are still required in your seven-card hand to make the Peasants become wild.

The Hope Diamond: If a player has the Ace of Diamonds, he cannot win unless all other players fold. If it makes him feel any better, all of his Aristocrats are secretly alive. This game is so named because the Hope Diamond is the least aptly named jewel in history. Owners such as Marie Antoinette came to conspiratorially celebrated ruin, as you will when this glittering jewel is found in your hand.

FUSION

Seven Card Stud. A pair can be combined to form a single wild card. For example, a player with a pair of 8s and a Queen can form the 8s into a single wild card and thus have a pair of Queens.

CLARIFICATION: Players love to ask stupid questions about this game. For example, Jeff asks, "I have four 9s and an Ace. Can I combine each pair of 9s into a wild card and have a pair of Aces with a Jack, but then form the pair of Aces into a Jack, then fuse the Jacks into a 2?" Yes, you can. Nice hand, Jeff.

GIMPSEY-DOODLE

Any game can have a Gimpsey-Doodle: It's just a special hand, declared by the dealer. Before the deal, the dealer calls out any specific set of cards (such as "the red 9s, the red 10s, and the 3 of Clubs"). This hand is the Gimpsey-Doodle, and is the best possible hand in the game.

BACKGROUND: A Gimpsey-Doodle is what we call any stupid collection of useless cards. We took it from the comic book *Cerebus*, in which the titular aardvark finds himself playing a stupid card game he doesn't understand with a bunch of sheltered schoolgirls, whom he also doesn't understand. You'll call Gimpsey-Doodle when your last hand was the worst hand imaginable, and you expect to be dealt it again.

GIRL'S BEST FRIEND

Five Card Draw. A heart is wild if it has a diamond to go with it.

CLARIFICATION: A player who holds one diamond and two hearts can make just one heart wild. It takes two diamonds to make two hearts wild, and you can't possibly make three hearts wild, since you only have five cards. The diamonds don't change themselves; they just enable the hearts to become wild.

BACKGROUND: This game was originally played with different suits, and was named after an uplifting work of poetry recited in a *Saturday Night Live* skit by the inimitable Tyrone Greene (a.k.a. Eddie Murphy). It is, believe it or not, too politically incorrect to print in this book, but with a little online research you can probably work it out. Here's a hint: It starts with "C."

GOOD COP, BAD COP

Seven Card Stud, with a maximum of six players. Nine cards are dealt in the center, in two rows of four cards, with the ninth card in the middle at the end. Before each betting round, a pair of cards is exposed, one from each row. Cards in the top row ("Good Cops") are wild, as are others like them, and cards in the bottom row ("Bad Cops") are dead, as are others like them. Deadness takes precedence over wildness, so if a card is both wild and dead, it's just dead. The ninth card, revealed before the last betting round, is the "Rizzo," and any player with a card of that rank is out of the game. When the Rizzo is revealed, a player with a matching card must immediately show that card and fold. If the Rizzo kills everyone, all players (not just live ones) re-ante and redeal.

BACKGROUND: Brought to us by the same Philadelphian who gave us Wide Goal Posts for Acey-Deucey, this priceless diversion from real poker features a glaring factual mistake. The Rizzo is presumably named after Philadelphia's Mayor Frank Rizzo, the rocket scientist who once said, "The streets are safe in Philadelphia. It's only the people who make them unsafe." The Rizzo's deathly nature probably refers to the mayor's bombing of a neighborhood to wipe out some terrorists, which had the unfortunate but completely predictable side effect of also wiping out the neighborhood. Hilarious indeed, except it was actually a different Philadelphian mayor, Wilson Goode, who did that. Nonetheless, the "Goode" is a terrible name for that card, so the name "Rizzo" sticks and history is once again rewritten through bad jokes and witty poker games. Sorry about that, Frankie.

VARIANTS: For goodness sake, don't change the rules. They're perfect. But you might be tempted to make the game more relevant to your own subculture by injecting a different cast of characters, such as baseball teams or hobbits. Call it what you will; by any name, Good Cop, Bad Cop is the next best thing to bobbing for mice.

GOOD SAMARITAN

Players receive hands of seven cards, followed by a betting round. Then each player must place two of his cards facedown in front of the live player to his left. These cards are not in the receiving player's hand, but they do make all cards of those ranks wild in that player's hand. Players examine their gifts, there is a second round of betting, and then high hand wins.

BACKGROUND: Jesus's story of the Good Samaritan lacks some of the punch that it no doubt had for his original audience. Back in the day, when every vicious desert tribe fought every other vicious desert tribe, one of the few things that everybody could agree on was that the Samaritans were worse. They would stab you in the back, sell your children, burn your tent, molest your live-stock, and force you to eat a ham and cheese sandwich. So when Jesus causes his questioner to acknowledge that a Samaritan is a worthy man, he is not just telling us that we must judge a man by his actions, but that *any* man may have the capacity for good. Even a Samaritan. (To get a better idea of where Jesus was coming from, imagine the parable is called "The Good Nazi." Ah, did that make your brain hurt? Good. Now we're on the same page.) Thus we can see just how appropriate this game's name is, as while in theo-ry everyone is trying to destroy you, you can actually win, thanks to the actions of one of your enemies. So when you win, don't gloat, or Jesus might smack you upside the head.

THE GOOD, THE BAD, AND THE UGLY

Seven Card Stud. When the second upcard is dealt, a card is dealt faceup in the center. Cards of that rank are wild (it's the "Good"). After the third upcard is dealt, a second central card (the "Bad") is dealt, and cards of that rank are dead. After the fourth upcard, a third card (the "Ugly") is dealt in the middle, and anyone with an upcard of that rank is out of the hand. The final card is dealt facedown, there is a final betting round, and the best hand wins. Note that you can win even if you have a downcard that matches the Ugly; it's only when they are face-up that they hurt you.

BACKGROUND: This game is sort of a nicer version of Good Cop, Bad Cop, and might have been its grandfather. As savory as the Rizzo story is, we frankly prefer the lasting image of Clint Eastwood shooting innocent fruits and vegetables out of a tree in New Mexico. Or Italy.

The Big Ten: GUTS

A lot of poker games require intestinal fortitude. In fact, a lot of poker games are even called "Guts." Turns out, it's one of the most overused names in the lexicon of poker, and just about everyone has a vastly different game they call "Guts." All these games can't possibly have come from the same source. So, it's been our privilege to choose from among them one game that we feel best represents the Platonic ideal. Which is, we assume, the replacement of crafty bluffing and shrewd calculation with hamfisted stubbornness.

Each player gets two cards, looks at them, and holds them face-down a few inches over the middle of the table. The dealer announces, "1–2–3–Drop!" and on the word "Drop," players either drop their cards or hold on to them. Those players that held on to their cards are "in," the others are "out." The in players show their hands, and whoever has the high hand wins the pot, while those who stayed in but lost must match the pot. The game is redealt and everyone re-antes. This continues until only one player goes in, at which point he wins the pot and the game is over. A player who drops out on one round is still in for the next. If no one goes in, the cards are collected and a new hand is dealt. If there is a tie, both players lose and pay the pot.

BACKGROUND: This is a game for when your brain wants some time off, some peace and quiet after too many rounds of

Johnny Mnemonic or Frankenstein. Two Card Guts, our choice for best Guts game, is sometimes called *Bullets*. This happens to be the name for the highest possible hand (two Aces).

STRATEGY: There's no real bluffing in Guts, which makes it either beloved or scorned depending on your personality and your blood alcohol level. People often erroneously call what you're doing in this game "bluffing" because they don't understand the philosophical difference between claiming you have a gun in your pocket and hitting someone with a bat.

VARIANTS: Guts is often played Lowball, but since you're just comparing two cards it's pretty much the same game one way or another. The only way to change the order of hands is to confuse people about what's good, by adding more cards.

There are many methods of declaring who's in. Some players like to take a chip under the table, and either bring it up or leave it below to indicate in or out. Some people keep their cards if they're out, and drop their cards if they're in. You can use sequential declaration ("check" or "in" until someone's in, "in" or "out" when someone's in), but you must rotate who goes first if you're going to do this. And by then you're playing a different game.

Guts with a Drop Penalty: First things first, let's punish the people who play conservatively. In some versions, if all the players drop out, the highest hand among the dropouts must match the pot. That'll serve you right for dropping that Jack–10.

Guts with a Gutless Ante: Instead of all players re-anteing after each hand, only those who dropped out must ante. This builds the pot more slowly and hurts the conservative players, though not as much as the drop penalty. Heck, you should probably use them both.

Putz: A common addition to Guts games is a kitty. This is an extra facedown hand that the winner of the game must beat in order to win the pot. If the winner can't beat the kitty, he's considered to have lost and must match the pot (and is called the "putz" by everyone else).

One Card Guts: As stupid as this sounds, it's really just a simpler version of the same game. There will always be somebody with the best hand, no matter how many or how few cards you deal. This just makes it easier to figure out where you stand. And more likely that you will have ties.

Monte Carlo: Three Card Guts. The third card adds more "variety," but as mentioned above, there's always going to be one player who's got a better hand than everyone else. You could play the game with ten cards if you wanted. To further muddle this "variety," some players like to play with the following three-card hands: high card, pair, flush, straight, three of a kind, and straight flush. (Note the position of the flush and straight. See Chapter Two for why.)

Progressive Guts: Players get two cards for the first round, then get an additional card for a second round, then a fourth card, then a fifth card, and then the hands are discarded and the game is redealt. When players are in, they compare cards secretly so that players who aren't in don't know what they have for later rounds. If you drop on one round, you're still in for the next. *See also* Legs *and* 3–5–7.

Spit Guts: A center card is turned faceup before each hand. Cards of that rank are wild. Again, with no betting rounds, this only serves to make it harder to figure out how good your hand is.

Guts Draw: Players get three cards. They may exchange up to two cards before having to declare. This actually adds strategy to the game, if you like that kind of thing. But as far as we're concerned, that way lies madness.

HAMLET

Seven Card Stud. Jacks are low, Queens are wild, and Kings are dead.

CLARIFICATION: Low cards are still cards, they just rank below all other cards and can't be used in straights (thus, the highest straight in Hamlet goes to the 10). Dead cards, on the other hand, are not in the game at all.

BACKGROUND: Based on the famous movie with Kenneth Branagh. When calling this game it's important to make dramatic gestures. When you say that Jacks are low, for example, you should hold your wrist to your forehead as if brooding and melancholy. Shake your hands and waggle your tongue for the wild Ophelia. (We *get* that she's not a queen, Bard buffs. Stop writing us.) Run your finger across your throat for the dead King, since being stabbed and poisoned doesn't have an internationally accepted hand gesture, but "dead" does.

VARIANTS: Hamlet can be played as Five Card Draw, and it's not bad Lowball. *See also* Rosencrantz and Guildenstern for the dreaded "Follow the Hamlet" game.

APPROVED INTERNATIONAL SIGN LANGUAGE METHOD FOR CALLING **HAMLET**

KINGS ARE **DEAD**   QUEENS ARE **WILD**   JACKS ARE **LOW**

Hamlet Meets the Three Stooges: This is Hamlet, played as Five Card Draw, with three "Stooges" dealt facedown in the middle (see The Three Stooges). After the deal, draw, and second betting round, the first of these facedown cards is revealed, and is wild (as are others of that rank). There is a round of betting. The second card is revealed, and is a community card (that is, it can be used in everyone's hand). Another round of betting. The third card is dead, as are others like it, unless it is a King, in which case it is the "Ghost of Hamlet's Father" and brings all Kings back to life. (Hint: If you have three Kings, don't count on them coming back to life.) A fifth round of betting follows the dead card, and then players spend the length of Hamlet's "slings and arrows" soliloquy figuring out what they have.

HEAVEN AND HELL

Each player gets five cards. Two rows of five cards are dealt facedown in the center. There is a betting round. Then one card from each row is turned over. Cards in the top row ("Heaven") are community cards, and can be used in everyone's hand. Cards in the bottom row ("Hell") are dead, as are other cards of that rank. There's a betting round after each set of cards is revealed, and then the next two cards are flipped, and so on until all ten cards are faceup. Players then make their best hand out of their own five cards and the cards in Heaven.

BACKGROUND: This game makes people twitch. Not the truly virtuous, of course. They know there's a grand design with their name on the blueprint. The rest of us suffer in solitary horror, not certain if our actions will bear us to a greater place or a fiery interment. This game should tell us, but we're sure it couldn't be that obvious.

VARIANTS: Some play with Heaven cards wild rather than

communal. Also when Heaven cards die, you can make them "angels," replacing them with fresh cards from the deck until they're alive again. This will guarantee that there are always five cards in Heaven.

The Divine Comedy: Between Heaven and Hell, there's Purgatory, a middle row of five cards. Cards in Purgatory aren't in anyone's hand, and aren't especially significant. They just stay on the board reminding you that you can't have them. Oh, and giving you critical information around which to craft your paradigm-shattering strategy.

HEINZ 57

Seven Card Stud. 5s and 7s are wild. If you get a wild card faceup, you must match the pot or fold. Facedown wild cards are free.

BACKGROUND: This game came very close to making the Big Ten, since it's got simple rules, eight wild cards, and a thrilling lack of fairness. In case you were wondering about the name, see, Heinz makes these 57 varieties of ketchup, and so, you know, 5s and 7s are wild. And ketchup is good for you.

STRATEGY: Because of the pot doubling aspect, 5s and 7s become more than just wild cards. They become forces of nature. If you're playing along with a weak hand and a large pot and you get a 5 faceup, you have to decide whether those three 8s are worth 12 dollars. When a number of players have faceup wild cards, they develop proprietary feelings for the pot, and thus are less likely to fold. Thus, this game is an instrument of divine retribution. We've seen people get three 5s up, pour barrelfuls of change into the pot, and be blasted by a natural straight flush. Retribution for what, you may ask? It must have been *something* pretty terrible, or else one is forced to assume that this is a cold mechanical universe devoid of higher justice.

VARIANTS: There is an obvious positional advantage in Heinz 57, but it's such a classic game that we don't really want to fix it. The first wild card in the game is so much cheaper than the last one that it's not adequately compensated by the fact that the last player knows a lot more when he gets his. With eight wild cards, this game can theoretically have a pot that doubles eight times. If you'd like to foil the positional advantage, start each dealing round with the high hand. But like we said, it's hard to meddle with perfection like this . . . unless you're Jeff.

Heinz Fixed-y Seven: The price of the pot-match is fixed at the beginning of the dealing round. This means that the pot is counted before each dealing round, and a wild card received at the end of this round costs the same as one received at the beginning. The "fixed" in Heinz Fixed-y Seven means "staying the same," not necessarily "better." But your group may appreciate the savings.

HIGH FENCES

Seven Card Stud. The winner splits the pot with the live player to his left.

CLARIFICATION: When this game is down to two players, it's over. Or, if you prefer, these two can play on hoping that the pot isn't evenly divisible, in which case they can waste everyone else's time battling over the odd nickel.

BACKGROUND: This game's title is derived from the maxim, "High fences make good neighbors." Note in the description the word "live" modifying "player." Players who have folded can't win the game no matter where they're sitting. Trying to bully someone out of a winning seat is only possible if a lot of alcohol has been consumed by that player, it is very late in the evening, and there is a live parrot loose in the house. Note the word "live" modifying "parrot."

HOUSE OF COMMONS

Seven Card Stud. The most common upcard is wild. If there is a tie for most common (there usually is), then it's the highest card among them. For example, if there are two 7s and two Aces showing, Aces are wild.

CLARIFICATION: The last legal time to fold is when the action is on you, and you owe money to the pot. This is the case in any game where one person's fold can steal the win away from one player, and hand it to someone else.

BACKGROUND: The British House of Commons has long been an international symbol of the power of representational democracy in the hands of the common man, and how it can be continually thwarted by an entrenched aristocracy. We seem to like this theme: see Socialism and French Revolution.

HURRICANE

Two Card Draw High-Low.

CLARIFICATION: You can draw up to two cards. The highest hand is a pair of Aces, and the lowest will depend on your house definition of Low, but from the era of the game, we'd guess it's a 32.

BACKGROUND: Hurricane was insanely popular in World War II, but not so much today. Maybe they had to cram a lot of people around a precious few tables, what with wood rationing and all. Maybe it's great even with a deck that's lost half its cards.

VARIANTS: Quite often played with Deuces wild.

Games That Aren't Poker: INJUN

Also knowed as "Injun Poker" and "Indian Poker." This is a classic, in the way that the AMC Pacer is a classic.

Each player receives just one card, which he cannot look at. Instead he holds it to his forehead (sticking it there with sweat, usually) so all other players can see it. A betting round ensues, and then the high card wins. No kidding. Please remain seated.

BACKGROUND: Okay, maybe we're a little hard on Injun. After all, despite its horrible name, it's a game with a long and respected tradition. Perhaps a good player can tell by the looks in his enemies' eyes and by the way they bet exactly what his own card is. Perhaps there are no reflective surfaces in your house and cheating is out of the question. Or perhaps our playtesters just haven't yet managed to drink enough tequila.

VARIANTS: Texas Hold 'Em played Injun-style is called Blind Man's Bluff. The name comes from the ancient game Blind Man's Buff, also known as Harass the kid with the Bag on his Head.

Mexican Sweat: Five Card Stud, dealt 1 "down" and four up. Each player puts their downcard to their forehead as in Injun, and it remains there until the hand ends. Not related to Mexican Stud at all, and presumably named after the copious perspiration required to stick a card to your forehead for three minutes, but at least it's a bit more of a poker game than straight Injun.

IRISH

Omaha. Each player is given four cards, but must discard two cards after the flop. This means that both the player's two hole cards must play in his final hand.

VARIANTS: Can also be played as Omaha-8 or as a Hold 'Em variant, meaning that a player need not use both hole cards in the showdown. Pineapple is also called Irish, mostly by folks in the UK.

JACKS OR BETTER

Five Card Draw. A player must have a pair of Jacks or better to open the betting on the first round. If no one opens, everyone re-antes and the hand is redealt, moving the deal one player to the left.

CLARIFICATION: In the showdown, it may be necessary to prove that you had the requisite cards to open. Usually this is easy, as they will play in the winning hand. But once in a while you are forced to "split your openers," such as throwing one Jack out of the pair to draw to a flush. In this case, it's necessary to declare that you're splitting your openers and keep your discard to the side, so that you can prove that your opening bet was legitimate at the showdown. Of course, this betrays the quality of your hand, so to be perfectly unreadable you should do this every time whether you're really splitting your openers or not.

BACKGROUND: This game is sometimes called *Jackpot* or *Jackpots*, since you need Jacks to open the pot. But that makes it sound more exciting than it really is, which, when you come right down to it, is a fairly mellow version of poker. A Jackpot, by comparison, is what one unerringly fails to win on every visit to a casino.

VARIANTS: Nearly any Five Card Draw game can be augmented by this rule. The purpose of the opening requirement is to prevent crazy freaks from opening on any darned thing, so if you're prone to playing with crazy freaks, this is a good weapon to keep in your arsenal.

Bobtails: A bobtail is a colorful antique term for a four-flush or an open-ended four-straight. These hands are added to the list of legitimate openers. Again, if you split one, make sure you keep the cards where you can prove you had them.

Progressive Jackpot: If no one opens, the opening requirement raises to a pair of Queens or better on the following deal.
(This makes sense, since the pot now has two antes from everyone.) If no one can open in the second round, the requirement
becomes a pair of Kings or better in the third. In the fourth
round, it's Aces. Then, as if computing the next highest hand
above two Aces was impossible (hint: it's two pair), the opening
requirement drops back to Kings, then Queens, then Jacks.
Presumably from there it bounces back up again, though we've
never made it far enough to check.

JACKS TO OPEN, TRIPS TO WIN

Five Card Draw, using the opening requirement from Jacks or
Better. In addition, to win, a player must have three of a kind
or better in the showdown (assuming it gets that far). If no one
can win the showdown, the remaining players re-ante and play
a new hand, passing the deal one player to the left.

VARIANTS: If no one can show a winning hand, you can
allow everyone another draw, limited only by the size of the
undrawn deck. Or you can reshuffle the discards after every
draw, offering unlimited re-draws after every failure to win. But
this is really no better than just dealing a new hand to everyone who's left in the game.

Super Progressive Jackpot Trips or Better: If no one opens, the
opening requirement goes up as it does in Progressive Jackpot.
The win requirement is always trips.

JOHNNY MNEMONIC

Seven Card Stud. After the deal, players must memorize their
first two cards, because after the first betting round they may

not look at these cards again. To win, you must be able to name both cards, by rank and suit, before you reveal them. This is true even if everyone else has folded; if no one wins, the pot remains, everyone re-antes, and the game is dealt again.

BACKGROUND: People rarely forget their cards once they know the rules, but we really like this game, and not just for the Gibson title. It sharpens our minds for casino play, where you really should memorize your freakin' downcards. In a casino, you should never look at your downcards because you have to, only because you want to.

VARIANTS: You can play this game "full-contact." Don't be shy. Shout out the names of random cards, even cards that don't exist, for the duration of the game. This game is extra fun when everyone spends the entire time shouting things like "Queen of Nines!" and "Blue of Spades!" and asking each other really hard math questions.

Memory Crash: If the winning hand fails to name his cards correctly, no one wins. Instead, the player who miscalled the winning hand must match the pot, and the game is redealt to the live players.

Doctor Allcome: Same as Memory Crash, but the pot-matching penalty applies to any player in the showdown who can't remember his cards, whether he has the best hand or not. If the winner knows his cards, the forgetful players pay him the amount in the pot and he also takes the pot. This will teach the lazy players to take this ridiculous game seriously.

JUNCTURE OF DESTINY

Seven Card Stud. Before shuffling, the dealer cuts the deck and reveals two cards of different rank. (The dealer re-cuts if this doesn't happen on the first try.) For each player, either one of these cards, but not both, can be wild. For example, if 2s or 7s are wild, this means that each player can choose either 2s or 7s as the wild card for his own hand.

BACKGROUND: "Juncture of Destiny" is Jeff's phrase for any strategic choice that takes someone too long. It's his way of reminding you that he, too, would someday like to take a turn.

KANKAKEE

Seven Card Stud. Each player gets two down cards, and a Joker is dealt in the center. The Joker is everyone's third card, and is wild. After this point, the game proceeds as Seven Card Stud.

BACKGROUND: Named for the Illinois riverboat gambling mecca. Apparently, Kankakee is home to a lot of eight-player tables of Seven Card Stud . . . where they all stay in. But we'd like to ask the, um, Kankakeeneans: Why use a Joker? Why not just say, "Everybody has an invisible wild card?" We suspect that there is no answer. But that's the way it's done and we're not gonna argue with tradition.

KNOCK

Each player places an ante before him (not in the pot), and receives a hand of five cards. One card is turned faceup and placed beside the deck, forming the start of a discard pile. Starting with the player to the dealer's left, each player may either draw or knock.

"Drawing" means taking either the top card of the discard pile, or the next card on the deck, then discarding one card on top of the discard pile, faceup. Kind of like you do in rummy.

To "knock" signifies that a player is satisfied with his hand, and is ready to show down. Every other player has one last opportunity to draw (or stand pat), and may also perform a third action, surrender. Surrendering means withdrawing from the game and immediately paying your ante to the knocker.

After all players have taken one of these options, the knocker is "called" and must show his hand. This is true unless all players have surrendered. If the knocker beats all the live players, each of them pays him twice the ante (their original bet plus the same amount again). If he is beaten by even one player, he pays twice the ante to *every* live player, and so does every other player who stayed in with a lower hand.

CLARIFICATION: Here's an example of five players playing Knock. Dave knocks, and Chris stays in, but Bob has the best hand. Alice and Egbert have surrendered, and have already paid 1 ante to Dave. Dave and Chris pay twice the ante to Bob. Dave and Chris also pay each other the same amount. Dave actually breaks even despite losing the hand, and Bob comes out 4 antes ahead.

BACKGROUND: Knock is actually a primordial precursor of poker, part of the string of games that demonstrate, almost convincingly, that poker is evolved from rummy. You should try this game if only to come to the same conclusion that pretty much everyone else has, namely that now that we have poker, we don't need this.

LEGS

You will need a button and at least three "leg" markers per player. (Use bottlecaps, if you are drinking from bottles. Or bottles, if it comes to that.) Each player is dealt two cards. After looking at the cards, each player holds them out, facedown. The dealer announces, "1–2–3–Drop!" and on the word "Drop," players must either drop their cards or hold onto them. Those that held on to their cards are in. The "in" players show their hands to each other in secret, vying for lowest hand. Every player in this exchange pays the amount in the pot to every player with a better (lower) hand. This means that if you are beaten by three players and there is a dollar in the pot, you pay a dollar to each of those players.

If only one player stays in, he earns a leg. It takes at least three legs to win the game. If no one stays in, no one wins anything, and the game moves on.

All players keep their hands, even those players who dropped out. Everyone re-antes, and a third card is dealt to each player. Drop cards and resolve as before (those who were out before can be in this time), but on this round the highest hand wins. This repeats with a fourth card, playing for low, and the fifth card, playing for high.

After the fifth card, the game is redealt. This cycle repeats until one player has earned two more legs than anyone else, with a minimum of three legs. That player wins the game and takes the pot.

VARIANTS: *See* Guts *and* 3–5–7 for some other ways to play this game.

LEROY

Seven Card Stud, Jacks are wild. Anyone showing a pair of Kings or better must immediately pay a dollar to each other live player, or fold. If a hand that has already paid becomes substantively better (i.e., moving from a pair to trips), it must pay again.

BACKGROUND: Named for the ol' stud horse in Big & Rich's *Save a Horse (Ride a Cowboy)*, the promo song for the 2004 World Series of Poker. It begins, "Well I walk into the room, passin' out hundred dollar bills. . . ." So technically, the penalty should be $100 a player, but that's a bit steep for a nickel game. You can even lower the price to a quarter if you're not so big and rich. But hey, your friends all have cable. They can afford a dollar.

LINCOLN

Omaha or Omaha-8. A player has the additional option of using only one of his cards and four on the board.

BACKGROUND: There are other cities in Nebraska, it turns out, and we imagine they're subtly different from Omaha. So too here. Unlike in Omaha, if the board comes 10♠–J♠–K♠–A♠ in this game, you can use your Queen of Diamonds to make a straight. Good luck with that.

LIZ TAYLOR

Seven Card Stud. Before shuffling, remove the Queen of Hearts and place it in the center of the table. That's "Liz." Whenever a player gets a faceup Jack or a King, Liz moves into that player's hand, and is wild. Each round, if a player has the Queen of Hearts, start the deal with that player instead of the dealer's left.

BACKGROUND: This game is obviously named for the violet-eyed starlet who's always been lucky in love. If your players enjoy a bit of role-playing, then Liz Taylor will provide ample opportunity for it. There will much talk of betrayal, and the fickleness of love, and, in a good game, several rounds of "I knew you'd crawl back to me, you tramp." This sort of thing happens regardless of the gender of the players.

VARIANTS: You can call the Queen anything that makes sense to you. Surely there is someone worthy of consideration in your immediate circle of friends.

Everybody Loves Liz: Queens are wild. When any Queen is dealt faceup, all faceup Jacks and Kings move into that hand. Any player with more than one natural Jack or more than one natural King can't win the showdown. (Note that this condition doesn't kill the player outright, so if your extra Jacks and Kings are in the hole, you can still bluff your way to victory.) To avoid positional advantage, start each deal with the highest hand showing.

THE LORD OF THE RINGS TRILOGY

This is a set of three Seven Card Stud games which can be played alone, in sequence, or compressed into a single game. The three parts are:

The Fellowship of the Ring: Red 9s ("the Fellowship") are wild. Black 9s ("the Ringwraiths") are dead. See, there are nine fellows in the fellowship, and nine black riders in the darkness. So, there you have it.

The Two Towers: The high hand ("Isengard") splits the pot with the hand with the most black cards ("Mordor"). All seven of your cards count for your Mordor hand, including the black 9s, even if they're dead. In the event of a tie for Mordor, the best all-black poker hand wins the tie.

The Return of the King: If a player is dealt a King ("Aragorn") faceup, he must "return" it. The King is discarded and not replaced.

The Whole Freakin' Epic: Combine all three of these rules, if you have the nerve. We like to play the "Extended" version, which has all three rules in a game of Eight Card Stud, plus the rule that the King of Hearts down can summon other discarded Kings into your hand, and any player with a 2 or a 3 (a "hobbit") can refuse a black 9 and instead receive the next card in the deck.

The Big Ten: LOW HOLE WILD

Frequently miscalled as "Low Hold Wild" by players who just don't know what they're talking about, Low Hole Wild is a solid poker game with some tricky strategy at the end. What's more, it mixes nicely with pretty much any Stud game that's not already too freaky. Imagine, Hamlet with Low Hole Wild. Why, that makes Jacks good again!

Seven Card Stud. Each player's low hole card (the lowest among his downcards) is wild for him, as are others of that rank. Aces are high. Players may pay 50 cents on the last round to receive their last card faceup.

BACKGROUND: The dealer's choice equivalent of "comfort food," because after everyone has had a scary experience with Frankenstein or California Guts, more than likely the next dealer will call Low Hole Wild. We like this game so much that once we've played Low Hole Wild a time or two, we usually start announcing that players can buy their last cards faceup for 50 cents even in games where it doesn't help. Who knows? Someone might do it just for fun.

STRATEGY: Why would you want to buy your last card faceup? Well, suppose you have a 7–8 down, and another 7 up. This means that right now you have two wild 7s. If your last card is a 2, it will give you one wild 2 instead. The higher your wild pair, the smarter it is to take your last card faceup.

Because of the possibility of wild pairs, you can assume the winner will usually have more than just one wild card. Buy your last card faceup if there's any chance it will hurt you to take it facedown, unless you think you are unlikely to win no matter what you draw. At that point, it's better to take the free card and take your chances.

VARIANTS: Low Hole Wild is a big traditional favorite, with plenty of variants including *Mexican Stud* and *Low Chicago*

Low Hole Wild. This game is also playable as Five Card Stud, and is usually still called Low Hole Wild even when players have only one downcard. (The appropriate phrase is actually "hole card wild.")

Low Hole Wild Roll Your Own: Each player's first three cards are dealt facedown. The player decides which of them to turn up, and then the game of Low Hole Wild is rejoined. This can also be played as *Low Hole Wild Roll Your Own All Day Long*, in which case every round is dealt facedown and players roll up a card of their choice each time. This virtually guarantees that someone will have two or three wild cards by the end.

Jump Start: As Low Hole Wild Roll Your Own, except each player is dealt five cards facedown, and immediately must roll up three of them. The next card is dealt faceup, and the one after that facedown.

◆ *Games That Aren't Poker: MAGIC 8-BALL*

Is this poker? Don't count on it. Is it popular? Signs point to yes. Does that make it worth putting in this book? Reply hazy, try again.

Seven Card Stud. The winner is the player with the most 8s. Cards of ranks below 8 may be combined to form 8s, with Aces being treated as rank 1. For example, a 5 and three Aces makes an 8. Cards above 8 are worthless.

CLARIFICATION: Poker hands do you no good here. All that matters is how many 8s you can make. If you have a full house, 10s over 9s, curse your rotten luck and fold, fold, fold.

BACKGROUND: A meme is an idea that replicates itself through a culture. Some sociobiologists suggest that memes are, in a weird way, a form of life, in that they adapt over time in order to survive. If this is so, then the Magic 8-Ball meme has evolved protective coloration that allows it to survive. Everything about this game looks like poker—the dealing, the shape of the hands, the system of betting—but it is *not* poker. It has evolved a shape that allows it to exist, and spread to other players, within poker's natural ecological niche. Much like those flies that have evolved to look enough like honeybees that they can take up residence in bee hives. Only with 8s.

◆ **VARIANTS:** Believe it or not, we run across this game a lot. But since nearly half the cards are worthless, we suggest an improvement: Treat face cards as half a point, so two face cards equals a 1. Now only 9s and 10s are worthless.

MEXICAN STUD

Five Card Stud, hole card wild, roll your own all day long. Each player gets two cards down, and decides which to flip up. After a betting round, each player gets another downcard, and decides again which downcard to flip up. This continues until all players have four upcards. Your low card is wild, as are others of that rank.

CLARIFICATION: As with any roll-your-own game, it's important that everyone roll their cards at the same time, to prevent one player from using his catlike reflexes to rethink which card to reveal when he sees what other cards have been shown. However, unlike all other roll-your-own games, this one requires that you do this to the tune of the Mexican Hat Dance.

BACKGROUND: Frankly, we are at a loss as to why this game was called Mexican Stud. Possibly it was invented by someone in Mexico. The reason it will *remain* Mexican Stud around here is that on every round, players must flip a card to make it face up, and this, for fairness, *must* be done simultaneously. Therefore you need a signal to let everyone know when they *must* flip up their card. So as soon as the dealer has dealt the current card, he (and perhaps the rest of the table) sings a chorus of the Mexican Hat Dance. At the end of the song, there is a final "Olé!", and with this declaration, everyone *must* flip their cards. You cannot buy entertainment like this.

◆ *The Mexican Hat Dance*
Daaaaah-da da-da-da da-da-da da-dahh
Duh-da da-da-da da-da-da DA-da
Da-da da-da-da da-da-da da-daaah
Dada dadada dadada DAH! Olé!

We're aware that not everyone knows the words to the Mexican Hat Dance song. Neither do we, but this has never stopped us. Therefore, as one of the numerous services we are rendering to you, our readers, here is the version of the Mexican Hat Dance that has been sung at Phil's games for close to twenty years.

VARIANTS: A number of games are called Mexican Stud, but we think this one's the best. The rest involve stripping a bunch of cards out of the deck, which somehow floats too far outside the realm of poker for even us.

MISSION CREEP

Seven Card Stud. 2s start wild. Whenever a player is dealt a wild card faceup, he must immediately change the rank of the wild card up or down by one position. (Aces wrap.)

CLARIFICATION: Here's how it works. Player 1 has an Ace and 9 down. He gets a 2 faceup, which would normally be a pair of Aces. But instead he must change the wild by 1 in either direction, so he chooses the Ace. He now has a pair of 9s. On the next card dealt, Player 2 gets an Ace. She has two Kings down, so she changes the wild card to a King. She now has three Aces, and Player 1 no longer has any wild cards at all.

VARIANTS: 2s don't have to start wild. You can flip a random card for the starting wild, reshuffle, and then deal.

MISSISSIPPI

Seven Card Stud, no limit, dealt two down and five up. On the first round, the lowest card must open the betting (lowest by rank, and then by suit if necessary). The fourth and fifth cards are dealt together (that is, there's no betting round between them), and the seventh card is faceup. There is no limit to the amount you can bet, except the money you have on the table.

BACKGROUND: Seven Card Stud is not the greatest no-limit casino game. It takes a while, and players fold a lot. Mississippi (also called *Big River*) was invented to bring Seven Card Stud into the casino world. It hasn't hit, really, but it's still a decent game.

MULTIBALL

Seven Card Stud for three to six players. If a player gets a King or an Ace face up, he may trade it in immediately for two new upcards. If either or both of them are Kings and/or Aces, he may continue to trade one card at a time until he has no further options to do so.

BACKGROUND: Be sure to make the pinball machine sounds. There's some serious bluffing in this game, because if you don't take the trade, you're announcing you have at least a pair of high cards. Well, at least for a little while.

MUNCH

Choose any game that has been called this evening, and play it again without the wild cards.

CLARIFICATION: For example, in Heinz 57 Munch, you must still match the pot when you get a 5 or a 7 faceup, but those cards aren't wild. In Follow the Queen Munch, nothing is wild, including (and you have to point this out when it happens) a card that comes up after a Queen.

BACKGROUND: This is one of those games you call when you start getting punchy. There isn't a game in this book that's improved by having the wild cards made unwild.

NEMESIS

Before shuffling, the dealer cuts to a single card. Cards of this rank are "poison." The dealer shuffles the poison card back in, and deals four downcards to each player. A betting round follows, then three rounds of upcards, with a round of betting after each. Whenever a poison card is dealt, all upcards on the table must be discarded, and dealing proceeds as usual. Because of positional advantage, each deal starts with the high hand showing (if there is one) rather than with the player on the dealer's left. If the board has no upcards when betting begins, the betting starts with the hand to the dealer's left.

CLARIFICATION: For example, suppose the poison cards are the 4s. When a 4 is dealt, remove all upcards from the game, and continue dealing the round. If another 4 is dealt, remove all the upcards again. There will be a total of three dealing rounds regardless of the occurrence of poison cards, so it could be that some or all players have nothing but their downcards in the end.

You may wish to keep track of the dealing rounds with chips, because the board may not tell you.

BACKGROUND: The standby "One man's meat is another man's poison" comes from actual science, as beings from the same species react differently to different poisons. It is possible that somewhere in the world, someone can swallow dram after dram of strychnine, and that the Guinness Book has monitored it. In this way, a player might get two Aces down and win this game, even if all his upcards have been killed.

NEUTRON STAR

Five Card Stud, dealt one down, three up, and one down. Any red card can be used to "drag down" the rank of any single higher-ranking black card, converting that card to the red card's rank. For example, a 3 of Diamonds can be used to convert a Jack of Clubs into a 3 of Clubs. Aces are always considered high for this rule, regardless of color. Each red card in a player's hand can be used for this purpose, so if a player had two red 3s and two higher black cards, he could use the 3s to make both black cards into 3s, making four of a kind.

BACKGROUND: If you're among the class of people who believe the universe to be billions of years old and that Mankind evolved from a race of walking fish, you might also believe in something called a "neutron star," a ball of matter so dense that a teaspoon of it would, on the surface of the Earth, weigh about a billion tons. Neutron stars, so the theory goes, are created when what remains of an exploding star has collapsed under its own weight, to the extreme that the protons and electrons in the matter have no choice but to fuse into neutrons. This is about as believable as the notion that light can be simultaneously a particle and a wave, or that there exists a function in calculus which is both the integral and derivative of itself. Nevertheless, it makes a quaint basis for this fun game, in which higher cards can be forced to "collapse" by the powerful "gravitational attraction" of lower ones.

VARIANTS: Five Card Draw works just as well for this game, but be warned that adding more cards into the mix will dramatically increase the quality (and homogeneity) of the winning hands.

Black Hole: The best hand formed by the rules of Neutron Star splits the pot with the best hand using the opposite rules, namely that lower black cards can drag down the ranks of higher red ones. As the name implies, you may need an extra five minutes and a team of research scientists to determine what everyone has.

NIGHT BASEBALL

Seven Card Stud, No-Peekum. Each player gets seven cards facedown, and cannot look at them. 3s and 9s are wild, and 4s get you an extra card.

Starting on the dealer's left (or with a random player if you have anything resembling a soul), players must roll their cards one card at a time until they beat the best hand showing or roll their last card, and then there is a pause for a round of betting. 9s are free, but if you roll a 3 you must match the pot or fold. A 4 gets you another upcard if you choose to pay a dime, and if there are cards left in the deck.

BACKGROUND: This has the same basic rules as Baseball, which are different wherever you go, but it's played No-Peekum, because you're playing at "night." This makes it even more "fun." Like many of the most Neanderthal games in this collection, Night Baseball is inexplicably popular.

VARIANTS: See Baseball itself for a list of variations on the Baseball rules. To improve any No-Peekum game, you should have each player flip one card at the beginning. This not only establishes a random starting point, rather than always using the seat on the dealer's left, but it also alleviates the gut-wrenching futility of calling bet after bet before you've seen even one of your cards.

NIGHT OF THE LIVING DEAD

Seven Card Stud. If a player folds, he continues to receive upcards. If he gets a spade faceup, he's back in the game for free.

BACKGROUND: Based on the groundbreaking George Romero comedy. Despite the "coming back to life" aspect of this game, it's actually rather dull when played correctly. The reason is that the resurrection rule makes folding a very attractive option and keeps the pots relatively small, which is basically the opposite of the effect most nickel-ante games are designed to have. As it turns out, it's better when played as Night Baseball of the Living Dead.

NIGHT BASEBALL
OF THE LIVING DEAD

We're willing to break our strict alphabetical order rules to bring you this game, which requires understanding of the two games above. It combines Night Baseball, which is unreasonably brutal, with Night of the Living Dead, which is unexpectedly dull. The result is a playable, if weird, game.

Play Night Baseball as you normally would. (If you "normally" play Night Baseball, Lord help you.) If you fold, which any wise person would do immediately, you remain in the game and continue to roll cards when it's your turn. If you get a spade, you are back in the game for free. A hand must be alive to be considered the best hand at the table, so if the high hand is a pair of 10s and you've folded, when you pair your Queens without rolling a spade, you are not yet the leader.

CLARIFICATION: If you're dead, you're dead. So if you get a 3 when dead, it's free. If you get a 4 when dead, you can't get an additional card. When you're dead, no one has to beat your hand, and you don't cause a betting round to occur when you roll your last card. Of course, if you get the 3 of Spades, you're both back in the game and forced to match the pot or fold yet again.

If you're playing the version of Baseball where a 3 kills you, or any version where you have to match the pot or fold, you aren't made super-dead by these actions. You can still come back if you fold, and later turn over a spade. Really, this is the only way to enforce this rule that's even vaguely sane.

NO-PEEKUM

Five Card Stud or Seven Card Stud. Players are not allowed to look at their hands. Each player is dealt his entire hand, facedown, and starting with the player on the dealer's left, each player rolls cards until he beats the high hand showing, or runs out of cards; in the case of the first player, this will mean rolling one card. The high hand starts a betting round, and the next player in sequence takes the next turn. A betting round will occur after any player runs out of cards as well. Play proceeds until all cards are revealed, and the high hand wins.

CLARIFICATION: When one player rolls his last card and is still not the leader, there is a betting round anyway, led by the high hand. The player who clearly can't win will, of course, fold. The next cards will be rolled by the player on his left.

BACKGROUND: Also called *No-Peek* or *No-Peekee*. Because you don't know what you have, this game can be insanely frustrating. The same effect could be achieved by simply dealing cards to players as they require them, to a maximum of seven, rather than giving each player seven cards he can't look at. Yet somehow it seems "better" when you include the temptation to look. The worst part about this game is that the dealer (or whoever acts last in the first betting round) must tough it out through a full table's worth of betting before he gets to look at his first card. No-Peekum, therefore, is recommended only for players who lack the power to distinguish Good from Evil, which probably describes all of us when it's late enough.

One way to keep the dealer from screwing himself by calling this game (he's in the last position), and to remove a few betting rounds from the game, is to have everyone roll one card to begin, and then start the betting with the high card showing. This, at least, randomly assigns the position that will have to wait the longest to see the rest of his cards.

OCEAN'S ELEVEN

Seven Card Stud. Cards are dealt to the right (counterclockwise). There are two new hands: All reds (any five red cards) beats one pair, and three pair beats two pair.

BACKGROUND: This game takes its jokes from the George Clooney film, in which Brad Pitt ekes out a meager living cold-decking *Teen Beat* cover boys. Note that though there is an all-reds hand, there is no equivalent all-blacks hand. Also, yes, in the movie they're playing Five Card Draw, not Seven Card Stud, but dealing that game to the right makes even less of a difference and you'd never get three pair without cheating.

When you investigate the world of casino poker and journey inevitably into the poker rooms of Las Vegas, Reno, or Gardena, beware how vocally you assert the unequivocal superiority of the well-crafted Soderbergh remake over the plodding, disjointed original. You will instantly become the sworn enemy of nine out of nine wrinkled truck drivers and off-duty short order cooks at your 4–8 Omaha table. Instead, avoid the subject altogether and celebrate the unassailable quality of *The Sting*, by snarling "The name's Lonnigan, and don't you forget it" in a thick Irish brogue.

PA FERGUSON

Seven Card Stud. The highest upcard on the table and all cards of that rank are wild. The wild card changes whenever a higher card is dealt faceup, or when the highest card(s) fold.

BACKGROUND: Named for 1910s Texas governor James "Pa" Ferguson, an inveterate Bourbon Democrat and crook. When the wild card changes, it's said to be "impeached," just like ol' Pa Ferguson.

VARIANTS: This works with any Stud game, and might even work with Hold 'Em.

Ma Ferguson: When a player receives a wild card, the owner(s) of the current wild card may offer that player any amount to discard it. If he accepts, the new card is discarded (and not replaced), and the old wild card stands. Named for Mrs. Pa, Miriam "Ma" Ferguson. In 1924, she became the first woman elected governor in U.S. history, and generously pardoned over 100 hardened criminals per *month*. Mmm, Texas.

PETER PAN

Five Card Draw, Lowball. Jacks are limited wilds: They cannot be used as Jacks, but they can be used as either Aces, 2s, 3s, or 4s, at the player's option. Queens, on the other hand, are wild.

BACKGROUND: Once upon a time, there was a little boy who refused to grow up. He spent his days playing games with other little children and having magical adventures in a desert paradise called Las Vegas. But enough about James. This game is about Peter Pan.

PHONE SEX

Seven Card Stud, Queens are wild. A timer is set as the first card is dealt. A player who holds a natural 9–7–6 at the showdown collects, from each other live player, 50 cents for the first minute and 25 cents for each additional minute that the game has lasted.

CLARIFICATION: Players will delay the game to make themselves more money. You may choose whether to punch them in the face, add a rule about delaying the game, or laugh and give them another 25 cents. It all depends on your general disposition, and whether you plan to invite them back.

BACKGROUND: For a fleeting moment, phone sex lines (and other pay-to-call numbers) started with 976. We're only guessing what they must have cost in those days. We never called one. We swear.

PICK A PARTNER

This is a partnership game, so it's playable only with four, six, eight, or ten players. Each player gets five cards facedown and turns over one of them. The player with the highest card showing picks another player as a partner. The player with the next highest card showing (if he doesn't have a partner yet) picks the next partner, and so on. (You don't get to know the partners' hands before you pick them, naturally.) The rolled cards are then discarded.

Each partnership then combines its remaining eight cards and reduces them to the best three-card hand (no straights or flushes), discarding the rest. A round of betting follows, then each team rolls one card. There is another bet, then the second card is rolled, then another bet, and then the third card. The high hand splits the pot between its two owners.

A team's cards can stay in front of either partner, as long as that player is live. Players don't bet as a team, so if one player folds prior to the showdown, but his partner stays in and wins, the survivor takes the entire pot.

BACKGROUND: This fossil is an excellent game if you've got a group of people who don't know each other. A *very* interesting game if played with a group of Yakuza bosses who have sworn to destroy each other.

PINEAPPLE

Texas Hold 'Em. Each player gets three downcards, not two. A round of betting occurs. Then each player must discard one of his downcards. Then three community cards are flopped, then there's a second bet. Then a fourth central card is turned over, then there is a bet, then a fifth central card, then a final bet and showdown. As in Hold 'Em, each player may use any combination of his two downcards and the five cards in the center.

BACKGROUND: This is the missing link between Hold 'Em and Omaha. Well, it's not missing, since everyone knows about it.

VARIANTS: Any variant that can apply to Texas Hold 'Em, such as Eight or Better, works with Pineapple.

Crazy Pineapple: Instead of discarding one of his initial three cards before the flop, this discard occurs after the flop.

Super-Eight: Each player gets and keeps three cards facedown. In the showdown, the player may use any combination of his three cards and the central five.

Crazy Eight: Like Super-Eight, except that before the flop, each player just turns up one of his three, and it remains part of his hand.

Tahoe Pineapple: As Super-Eight, except a player can use no more than two of his three downcards.

PINOCHER

This is Poker played with a Pinochle deck (forty-eight cards, eight each of the Aces through 9s).

BACKGROUND: Basically, an offshoot of Bluff, the poker ancestor played with 10s through Aces and no straights or flushes. For extra fun, you can pronounce this game like the deposed Chilean dictator.

POINT AND SHOOT

Five Card Stud. After the final card has been dealt and the subsequent betting, the dealer calls "1–2–3–Point!" Each player must point to one of his own cards (up or down) that he wishes to replace. If a player wants to stand pat, he can point to the ceiling. Faceup cards are replaced faceup, downcards are replaced facedown. There is a final betting round, and then a showdown.

STRATEGY: If you have four hearts up, it's probably better to point to the ceiling even if you don't have a fifth heart down. This is true as long as the chances of people believing you have a flush are better than your odds of drawing a fifth heart, which start at 9 in 48. If you're a compulsive bluffer, however, you might as well be honest with yourself and take the draw.

POINTILLISM

Seven Card Stud. The high hand splits the pot with the hand with the highest number of pips.

CLARIFICATION: Your "pip" hand can only contain five cards, not seven, and the number of pips on a card is equal to its rank (you don't count the small ones in the corners). This means an Ace has one, a 2 has two, and so on through 10. Face cards are pipless. If you're playing with a nonstandard deck, you'll just have to pretend.

BACKGROUND: Named for the art technique of making pictures out of dots. Also known as *Midnight Train to Georgia*, after the popular song by Gladys Knight and the Pips. (She had three.)

PRAVDA

Five Card Stud. Before dealing each upcard, the dealer must ask the player if he wishes to "suppress" this card by paying 50 cents to the pot. Suppressed cards are dealt facedown. Because of positional advantage, each dealing round after the first starts with the high hand, rather than the hand on the dealer's left.

BACKGROUND: Pravda is Russian for "Truth" and was the name of the official newspaper of the Soviet Union, right up until the wall fell down, the Soviet Union broke up into a bunch of non-threatening city-states, and the newspaper staff quit and launched an online version, which now exists solely to disagree with the paper version.

The Big Ten: THE PRICE IS RIGHT

> ♦ We've been playing this game for years as Do Ya?, but our research seems to prove that it's actually called The Price is Right. This is borne out by the fact that there's another perfectly good game called Do Ya? and that the game called The Price is Right shows up in a lot of places and has pretty much these rules. By any name, it's a keeper, and manages just barely to squeak into our top 10.

Each player starts with two cards facedown. A button starts on the dealer. The dealer turns over a line of three cards beside the deck. Starting with player to the left of the button, each player in turn may choose to take the first card (the card farthest from the deck) for free, the second card for a nickel, the third card for a dime, or the unknown card on top of the deck for a quarter. When a player buys a card, a new card replaces it (that is, the nickel card is replaced by another card that costs a nickel; the rest of the line doesn't move). If a player buys the top card of the deck, he still adds it to his hand faceup.

After all players have bought a card, the remaining cards are discarded, and there is a betting round. The button moves one player to the left, and this series of events occurs four more times, until each player has five upcards. Then a final betting round occurs, and high hand wins.

BACKGROUND: It's difficult for us to square with the idea that a game called The Price is Right doesn't have oversized golf putters and yodeling mountain climbers, but this is a pretty solid game. Chances are, you've played some version of it at least once (maybe you even thought it up on your own).

STRATEGY: Pick a hand you want to make, and stick with it until a better idea comes along. Despite the temptation to play defensively, you can't win the game just by depriving another player of his third King. If you're not going to improve your hand by taking that King, just let him have it and stop kidding yourself. Jumping on a grenade to stop another player from winning is exactly as dumb as it sounds. Furthermore, as bad as the cards on the table look to you, paying a quarter for the card you can't see is almost always a bad investment.

VARIANTS: There are dozens of ways of dealing and pricing the cards. The game's occasionally played High-Low, and some players play that a card bought down stays down. (This is okay if you paid a quarter for it; not so good if it was free. See below.) Some groups play without a button, and let the high hand have first crack at each new deal; in other groups, a card isn't discarded until all players have a chance to buy it. This requires tracking this fact in some way, which we like to do with a bag of exploding beans and a talking duck.

Nickel Dime Quarter: Basically the same, except the cheap card costs a nickel, the second card is a dime, and the third card is a quarter. The top card off the deck is free. This turns on its head the "I'll pay extra to get a card that isn't any of those crummy cards" strategy, flipping it into "I'll pay nothing and take my chances on the unknown."

Abyssinia: Two cards are faceup, one on either side of the deck. Players buy cards as above, but the price is based on card's rank, not position in the line. You pay a nickel for a 2 through 9, a dime for any 10 or face card, and a quarter for an Ace. (The dealer can set these prices however he'd like.) The card on top of the deck, if you take it, is turned faceup and costs you the same price as if you'd bought it from one of the sides.

Wall Street: Four cards are faceup in the center ("Wall

Street"). The first card in the line costs a nickel, the second a dime, the third 15 cents, and the fourth 20 cents. You can't buy the top card of the deck. The big difference in Wall Street is that, when one card is bought, the other cards in the line slide down to fill the gap, and a new card is added in the 20 cent slot. For example, if someone buys the card that costs a dime, the 15-cent one slides into the dime spot, the 20-cent one now costs 15, and a new card is dealt into the 20-cent slot.

PROCTER AND GAMBLE

Each player gets four cards facedown. Three community cards are dealt facedown in the center. Players bet after receiving their first four cards, then one card is exposed, followed by a betting round, then another card, then another betting round. When the third card is exposed, that card and all others of its rank are wild. There is a final bet, and a showdown in which each player may use any combination of his four cards and the three in the center.

BACKGROUND: This is an old standard named for the well-known manufacturer of personal hygiene products, and the less-well-known manufacturer of artificial fat. Basically, we just like any game with "gamble" in the title.

PUSH

Five Card Stud High-Low. A button designates the dealer, and moves to the left with each deal. Each player in turn is offered a card and asked if he wants to keep it, or push it. If he keeps the card, the dealer moves on to the next player. If he pushes the card, that card goes to the next player, who immediately has the same choice. The card can be pushed all the way around the table, and if the last player doesn't want it, it's pushed into the middle of the table. Every player who refused the card gets a second card, and must keep it. This process continues until everyone has one upcard, and then there is a round of betting.

On the second dealing round, move the button one space to the left and start with the second player. The same pushing rules apply. Continue for four rounds, then show down for high and low hand.

BACKGROUND: Every now and then, you get a "grenade moment." Somebody gets a 7, say, and they push it. The next person pushes it, and the next, and then it comes to you, and the person after you already has an up 7, and there he is grinning like an idiot, telling you to push. Now heaven knows *you* don't want it, but all the delinquent previous owners are yapping at you like a pack of rat terriers telling you to hold on to it. Neither choice is palatable; after all, what did those slobs ever do for you? On the other hand, here's your chance to be a hero (admittedly, as far as heroing goes, it's on a par with opening a tight jar for your spouse, but the satisfaction of doing so has strengthened many a marriage), and how often do you get that?

VARIANTS: This is best as High-Low, with or without a declaration round, but is also playable as straight high. Push is also good with six cards, either dealt two down and four up, or one down, four up, one down.

Some players prefer the dealer to immediately fill a player's card after he pushes, rather than wait till all players have had the opportunity to push. A few players want to charge a quarter to push a card, but we like it better as a free push. After all, the game is called Push, not Think Seriously About Pushing, But Think Better Of It Considering The High Price Of Doing So.

Pushover: If the cards accumulated in the middle of the table win for either high or low, no one wins and the game is redealt to the surviving players.

Shove: If a player wants to keep a pushable card, the player to his right can pay a quarter to the pot and force the card to be pushed. The sequence of events goes like this: First, the dealer gives a card to a player. The player has the option to push it. He declines. The dealer then offers the same option to the player on his right, who can pay a quarter to push it. This may be a little tedious, but it's rewardingly cruel. For one thing, if the player didn't really want that card, he just tricked someone else into putting a quarter into the pot to get rid of it.

Push-Pull: Five Card Draw, with a push. If drawing cards, each player may see the first of his cards, and decide whether to keep it or push it for a quarter. You can't push any cards but this one so once a player pushes or keeps the first card, he receives the rest of his draw. A pushed card becomes the next player's first drawn card. This continues until the last player either takes his first card or pushes it, in which case the first player gets to see the pushed card before it before it is burned. Betting and showdown proceed as normal.

QUARTERBACK

Five Card Stud, Aces and 9s are wild. Players must ante an extra quarter, which they will get back (even if they lose) as long as they survive to the showdown.

BACKGROUND: Johnny Unitas, Mike's pick for the best quarterback of all time, was Number 19 in your Baltimore Colts program, hence the Aces and 9s. If you prefer Brett Favre, make 4s wild instead; if you have a soft spot for Joe Montana, then play Aces and 6s wild.

REMBRANDT

Seven Card Stud. Face cards are wild.

BACKGROUND: It's important to call the face cards "Picture Cards," or "Paint," since this makes an actual joke out of the title.

VARIANTS: In *Titian*, only the red face cards are wild. In *Louvre*, there are no wild picture cards, but the player with the most of them takes half the pot. In *Picasso*, 7s are wild, because they look nothing at all like people. Pretty much any joke you want to make up about art, now's your chance.

RESCUE 911

Five Card Draw. The "injured" cards (one-eyed Jacks and the suicide King) are wild. A *natural* 9–Ace–Ace beats every other hand.

CLARIFICATION: The one-eyed King (that's the King of Diamonds) isn't injured. He was born that way.

BACKGROUND: Remember when this was a TV show starring William Shatner? Well, we do. Because we named a game after it. Otherwise, we probably would have forgotten all about it.

VARIANTS: OK, you can make the one-eyed King wild if you want.

Rescue 911 with a Media Crew: All the discards become a single hand, the "Media Crew." After the showdown, the Media Crew makes its best five-card hand. If the winner doesn't beat the Media Crew, the pot stays and the hand is redealt, including only the surviving players. A hint: If you think you can't win, throw away 9s and Aces. This might give the Media Crew a 9-1-1, and force the game to repeat.

RIVER OF BLOOD

Texas Hold 'Em. If the "river" card (the fifth community card) is red, then the game continues. After the bet, another card is dealt, and another betting round occurs. If that card is red, another card is dealt, and so on until a black card is dealt and the final betting round occurs.

BACKGROUND: How can you not like a game called River of Blood? Actually, it's a little disappointing; half the time, the river isn't even red.

ROLL YOUR OWN

Seven Card Stud. Each player is dealt three cards facedown, and selects one to roll up. Players must roll their cards simultaneously. The game then proceeds as Seven Card Stud, with subsequent rounds being dealt normally.

VARIANTS: This game mixes well with Chicago, Low Hole Wild, or any other game where your downcards really matter.

Flip: Each player is dealt four cards and flips two simultaneously before the first betting round. The game then proceeds as Seven Card Stud.

Roll Your Own All Day Long: Same rules as Roll Your Own, but you get a downcard every round, and roll over a card every round. At the end, each player will have five cards faceup and two cards facedown.

Dakota: Low Hole Wild, Roll Your Own All Day Long, with a High-Low split. The lowest downcard in a player's hand is wild for high hand only, along with all cards of that rank. The seventh card is dealt facedown and will stay that way, unless the player opts to takes the faceup option for a dollar (*see* Low Hole Wild). You can decide whether you want to have a declaration round or not. By this point you've probably decided whether you like them.

ROSENCRANTZ AND GUILDENSTERN

A robust crossbreed of two prize studs, Follow the Queen and Hamlet. This game is played like Follow the Queen, except the card dealt after the Jack is low, the card dealt after the Queen is wild, and the card dealt after the King is dead. Since cards can occupy multiple states, there is a hierarchy of precedence: dead beats wild, and wild beats low.

CLARIFICATION: Jacks, Queens, and Kings are not themselves special in this game (unless one of them comes up after one of the others). If the last card dealt faceup is a (whatever), then no cards are (whatever that would make them). Don't be afraid to use scratch paper to track what's what. You think you won't need it, but you will. You will.

BACKGROUND: Named for the two knuckleheads who follow Hamlet around and eventually get their heads cut off cheaply and conveniently offscreen. This game makes about as much sense as the Tom Stoppard play, and it's just as funny.

SAN FRANCISCO

Seven Card Stud. Queens are wild, and straights don't count.

CLARIFICATION: "Straights don't count" means that a straight isn't a hand. It doesn't mean that if you have a straight flush that you don't have a hand, it just means that you only have a flush.

BACKGROUND: This is one of those ubiquitous games that is refreshingly easy to explain. It's about San Francisco, where, you know, they play cards differently.

SCHRÖDINGER'S CAT

Five Card Draw. 9s are wild. Before the deal, a card (the "Cat") is placed facedown in the center. After the second betting round, the Cat is revealed. All cards of the Cat's rank are wild. All cards of the Cat's suit are dead, except for the 9, which remains wild. There is a third betting round, and then the showdown.

CLARIFICATION: Let's say the Cat is the 5 of Clubs. That makes 5s and 9s wild, and clubs dead, except for the 9 of Clubs, which is still alive and wild. If the Cat is the 9 of Spades, then only 9s are wild, and Spades are dead, except for the 9 of Spades. Actually, the 9 of Spades is on the table, so it doesn't matter if it's dead or not. Hence, the name.

BACKGROUND: Schrödinger's Cat is named for the whimsical thought experiment by physicist Erwin Schrödinger. It involves a cat, a sealed box, and a canister of poison gas. See, in the wacky world of really, really smart people, if you put a cat in a box with a can of poison gas that might kill it, and might just as easily not kill it, you not only don't know whether the cat is alive or dead, but it's philosophically correct to describe the cat as being both alive and dead at the same time, until you allow enough time to elapse that the cat has either escaped to Bermuda or died of more a pedestrian cause, such as studying physics. This is fascinating if you are able to view the cat, the poison gas, and the box as mathematical abstractions rather than a cat, a can of poison gas, and a box, and to perceive the agent of this debacle as a lovable old man with a pretty good point, rather than a sadist who just put a cat in a box with a canister of poison gas.

Suitable detached appreciation of Schrödinger's experiment allows you to postulate that, without proof, God can both exist and not exist simultaneously, or that, once shuffled, every card in the deck is in every position in the deck until the top card is drawn and examined. Stephen Hawking once said, "When I hear of Schrödinger's cat, I reach for my gun." Some of your players may do the same.

SENSELESS VIOLENCE

Five Card Draw Lowball. A player must win twice (not necessarily in succession) to win the pot.

BACKGROUND: This game is similar to Legs, a guts game in which you must win more than once to actually win the pot. Any

---

♦ *Games That Aren't Poker: SCREW YOUR NEIGHBOR*

Screw Your Neighbor is a drinking game occasionally called by people who are unfortunately at the same table as poker players. The object of this game is not to get stuck with the lowest card. Aces are always low, and suits are irrelevant. Each player puts four antes (usually quarters) in front of him, and a button starts on the dealer.

In each round, each player receives one card. Starting with the player to the left of the button, each player may either keep his card or exchange it with the player on his left. The player on the button is special, and may exchange cards with the deck instead of the player on his left. Then all players reveal their cards, and the lowest card pays a penalty, such as taking a drink of harmless fruit juice, and paying an ante to the pot. If there's a tie for lowest card, the next lowest card pays instead. (That's the really clever bit.) Then the button moves to the left, the deck is reshuffled, and the game continues.

When a player loses his last ante, he is out of the game. When only one player remains, he wins the pot.

BACKGROUND: This is the drinking game that most resembles poker. Drinking games can involve anything from how many times Dr. McCoy says "He's dead, Jim," to how many volts of electricity you can take before you drop the electrodes. Tests of players' physical and mental acumen are pretty popular, as are counting things which, ostensibly, are outside any of the players' control. There are a million of them on the web, and they all end with, "You might not want to play this with your girlfriend."

VARIANTS: In many versions of this game, Kings are "stoppers," meaning they can't be traded for. Any player attempting to trade a card with the holder of a King is stuck with his current card, and the King is turned face up (usually after the trade has been attempted, to really rub that player's nose in his impending loss). Play resumes with the player to the left of the King.

We've also seen the simple rule that if there's a tie for lowest card, both players lose. Then everybody "gets" to kick in another ante and the fun resumes.

game that requires you to win twice is pretty nefarious, since even when you have no chance of winning you can easily be tempted to stick around and take you chances with the next hand. From a purely strategic angle, this is foolish. But as the new saw goes, you can have fun, gamble, or play smart, but not all three.

SEQUENCE

Seven Card Stud. If a 2 is dealt faceup, 2s become wild. If, once 2s are wild, a 3 is dealt faceup, 3s become wild instead. This can continue with 4s, 5s, and so on.

BACKGROUND: This game is like Follow the Queen, except that it's fairly easy to guess what specific cards will be wild by the end. In Follow the Queen, any card might be wild. In this game, starting with a 3 and a 4 in your hand is pretty exciting.

SHOTGUN

Five Card Draw, with extra betting in the beginning. Players are dealt three downcards, then a round of betting occurs, then players receive a fourth downcard, then bet, then a fifth card, then a bet. After this, players may draw normally as in Five Card Draw. A final betting round occurs, and the high hand wins.

VARIANTS: Shotgun High-Low is sometimes called *Skinny Minnie*.

Texas Tech: Also called *Double-Barreled Shotgun*, this is a

◆ *Games That Aren't Poker: 7–27*

This game is a little bit like Blackjack, and not very much at all like poker. Nevertheless, it's often encountered in a night of dealer's choice. At least it's slightly more like poker than Acey-Deucey.

Players will get two cards to start, and may keep taking more cards until they are satisfied. The goal is to get as close as possible (on either side) to 7 and/or 27.

Start by dealing each player two cards, the first up and the second down. Number cards are worth their rank, Aces can be used as ones or elevens, and face cards are worth 1/2. There is a round of betting, followed by a round of dealing in which each player may either take a card or stand pat. Each dealing round is followed by a betting round, and the deal continues until everyone stands pat. It is legal to stand pat on one round and still take a card on the next.

After the last bet, there is a showdown in which the hand totaling closest to 7 splits the pot with the hand totaling closest to 27. You can miss your total on either side, but if there is a tie for distance, the lower number wins. For example, a total of 6 1/2 beats a total of 7 1/2, because each is a half-step away from 7, and 6 1/2 is lower. The best possible hand in this game is 5–A–A, which has a total of both 7 and 27, and can win both ways.

VARIANTS: Often (and by "often" we mean, "we never play this, but when we do"), we play to 7 1/2–27 1/2, as that theoretically makes face cards more valuable. Because this is a split-pot game, it's possible to have a declaration round, if the dealer so chooses. Also, some houses rule that going over 27 busts you out, but that never made much sense to us. A 32 isn't going to win anyhow, so why penalize it further?

High-Low game. After the draw, players arrange their cards in the order they want to reveal them. Then all players roll one card, followed by a round of betting, then a second card, then a bet, then a third card, then a bet, then a fourth card, then the final bet. A declaration round occurs, and high and low hands split the pot. Some people also bet after the declaration, which makes for a total of nine betting rounds. The folks in Lubbock can't possibly have that much free time.

SLAUGHTERHOUSE-FIVE

Each player receives a hand of five cards, and five cards are dealt facedown into the center, in a collection of cards called the "slaughterhouse." All players expose one card from their hands, and then one card is exposed in the slaughterhouse, with all cards of that rank becoming dead. Then a betting round occurs. This occurs four more times. After the last card in the slaughterhouse is exposed and the last betting round, the cards are shown, and highest remaining hand wins. If no one has a hand, all players re-ante and the game is redealt.

BACKGROUND: Named for the mind-bending Kurt Vonnegut novel. Not really based on it, though. If it was, it would have to involve one card time-traveling back and forth between betting rounds. Trust us, we're very sophisticated game designers. If we could make that work, we would.

SOCIALISM

Seven Card Stud. All face cards are dead.

VARIANTS: Socialism can be played Lowball or High-Low, in which case your dead cards can be included in your low hand. (This is an exception to the usual behavior of dead cards, i.e., that they aren't in your hand at all.) The best Socialism low hand is five face cards.

SONNY & SHARE

Seven Card Stud. Jacks, Queens, and Kings ("Gypsies, Tramps, and Thieves") are wild, but the best hand using the wild cards must split the pot with the best natural hand.

BACKGROUND: Back before any of the authors were old enough to gamble (except Phil), a whimsical variety show featuring a starry-eyed elf and her adorable little goblin delighted a generation of poker players with music, controversy, and the occasional yo-yo act. Unfortunately, as far as we can tell, this generation never bothered to name a poker game after Sonny and Cher, so we did it for them. You can thank us when you meet us.

The Big Ten: SOUTHERN CROSS

> ♦ There are endless variations on the cross motif in poker, hardly surprising when you consider how much praying is begotten when the pot starts to swell. Personally, we've never noticed prayer help anyone for any length of time at the table, though we've seen many miracles, an unfortunate number of which were delivered unto the unworthy (i.e., anyone playing against us).

The dealer deals each player five downcards, and another set of five community cards facedown in the center, in a cross pattern. (These cards are dealt like a normal hand; i.e., one card after each player gets their first card, one after each gets their second, and so on.) A betting round occurs before any cards are exposed. The top card of the cross is revealed, and another betting round occurs. This continues with the right card of the cross, and so on with the bottom, left, and finally the center card, with a betting round after each. In the showdown, a player may use any combination of his five cards and *either* the three horizontal cards or the three vertical cards in the cross.

BACKGROUND: Also called *Criss-Cross, Iron Cross, Lacrosse,* and pretty much any other phrase with "cross" in it. This game is closely akin to Cincinnati, which has five community cards in the middle but no pattern restricting which cards can be used, and Tic-Tac-Toe, which is just this game taken to ridiculous extremes.

STRATEGY: Some part of the cross is going to make someone a pretty good hand. Watch how aggressively players are betting. If you've got a good read on a player, you can tell when they made their hand, and thus which portion of the cross they're using.

VARIANTS: All kinds of shapes can use this rule, if you're so inclined: Z's, H's, squares, fractals, whatever your demented mind can conceive. The trick is to come up with a pattern that contains smaller sets of cards. For example, the classic *X Marks the Spot* is just like Southern Cross, but in an X shape.

Fiery Cross: The center card, and all cards of that rank, are wild.

Holy Cross: Six cards are dealt in the center, with the sixth card at the bottom of the middle of the cross. The bottom card is the first to be revealed, then the left, then top, then right, then the lower central one, then the center. Players may use either the three horizontal or the four vertical cards. The sixth card means seven betting rounds.

The Passion of the Christ: This is the same as Holy Cross, but players will be "nailed" to the cross. This means you must either use all four vertical cards and one card from your hand; all three horizontal cards and two cards from your hand; or choose not to be crucified and use only the cards in your hand. (In the *Order of the Sacred Heart* variant, the center card and all of its rank are wild.)

The Ring: Same layout as Southern Cross, with a pivotal decision facing each player. Each player gets two hole cards. The central community card is wild, but a player may choose to use all four cards of the outer ring (none wild) instead of either crossing bar. Trouble is, there's a declaration round before the central card is flipped. After the bet following the fourth card, each player takes a chip below the table, and either brings it up (declaring that he is using the ring) or not (using one of the crossbars). This decision cannot be changed once the wild card is revealed.

Lucky 7: Seven cards are arranged in the shape of a 7. Each player gets three cards. The leftmost card of each leg is exposed after the first bet. The middle card on top and the two middle cards on the diagonal are exposed after the second bet. Then after the third bet, the upper right card is exposed, and it and all of its rank are wild. There's one more betting round, then each player may use either leg with his community cards.

Superstar: Each player gets a hand of five cards, and five more cards are arranged in the center like the points of a star. Before the first betting round, the top card of the star is exposed. The next clockwise card is exposed before the second bet, and so on around the star. Each player may use any combination of his five cards and two cards connected by a line of the star (that is, any two non-adjacent cards in the star). *Superstar of David* is the same game with the cards laid out as the tips of a six-pointed star, and an extra betting round for the sixth exposed card. *Pentagram* is like Superstar, but played for low, with the star dealt upside down and revealed in counterclockwise order.

Death Wheel: Each player gets four cards. Six cards are dealt facedown in a circle. Before each betting round, one card in the wheel is exposed (expose them in order, clockwise). At the showdown, players may use any three consecutive cards in the wheel plus their four downcards to make their best five-card hand. Sadly, there's no actual death involved.

SPIT IN THE OCEAN

Each player gets four downcards. While the dealer is dealing, one random player must call out "Spit!" The next card on the deck is flipped faceup in the center, and becomes a community card that is usable by all players. What's more, it's wild, and so are the other three cards of its rank. The dealing resumes and continues until the players have hands of four cards. There is a round of betting, then players may draw cards as in Five Card Draw, then there is a final round of betting and a showdown for high hand.

CLARIFICATION: If no one calls "Spit!" then deal the spit card at the end. Then get a new group of players.

BACKGROUND: Spit in the Ocean, or just *Spit*, is a game so well-known that many players call community cards "spit cards." Spit probably predates, and therefore gave rise to, the variety of games in this list that use community cards, like Cincinnati, Southern Cross, and even America's teenage sweetheart, Texas Hold 'Em, not to mention the assemblage of Spit variants below. It's a simple enough game and therefore a likely candidate to be requested when the dealer can't come up with a better game.

VARIANTS: People like yelling "Spit!", so why not play a bunch of variants and give them more chances to do it?

Pig in the Poke: The spit card is not wild, but all others of its rank are.

Wild Widow: The spit card is wild, but the others aren't.

Spitball: The player who opens the pot must win the game or match the pot. If the opener loses, no one takes the pot, the opener matches it, and the game is redealt to the surviving players.

Stormy Weather: A total of three spit cards must be called for during the opening deal, but are all dealt facedown. Players draw cards and then bet before the first card is turned, then bet again after that card is shown up, then again after the second, then again after the third. Player may use only one of the three cards in the center, and only the card he uses, plus the others of that rank, are wild for him.

THE STRIP

Texas Hold 'Em, with two rows of five community cards on either side of an imaginary Strip. The cards on both sides of the Strip are dealt in the same pattern as Hold 'Em, with the first three of both sides being flopped together, etc. Players make a hand for each side of the Strip, but may not combine cards from both sides. The pot is split between the best hands using each side of the Strip.

BACKGROUND: This game was once called *Double Flop*, but that's a terrible name. A game this good needs a real poker name, so we gave it one. The only downside is some confusion with a similarly named game.

◆ *Games That Aren't Poker: STRIP POKER*

This is supposed to be as complete a book of weird poker games as we could make it, so let's get it over with. If this is the game you bought the book for so you could introduce it to your regular Friday night game, you live a far more interesting life than we do, and that's saying something. This can be a fun little game when you're with a small number of close friends and perhaps some fruit juice. This game isn't poker because the incremental nature of betting has been gutted in favor of entertainment. The only correct reason to play is an esthetic one, i.e., to admire the grace and perfection of the unclad human body in an informal setting, so be cool, fool. The point is to get people naked, so if you are playing with strangers, care about your reputation, or are the daughter of any of this book's authors, this game isn't for you.

The best Strip Poker game is straight Five Card Draw. No ante. No wild cards. Draw two. Instead of money, you bet with articles of clothing. You can't fold. A losing player must remove an article of clothing. This is put to the side. The winner does *not* collect it. If a player who has lost an item of clothing wins, they may not put it back on. The last person to lose all their clothing is the winner, we guess.

Ideally all players should start with a similar amount of clothing. *Traditionally*, women are allowed a slight edge. Discussions should be held first to define what constitutes clothing. Does an earring count? Is it a bet of equal value to a shirt? Now we're outside the realm of this book. Heck, we might've started this section there.

SUCK

Three Card Stud, sort of, dealt one down and two up. There is a betting round after each card, including the first facedown card. If a player folds, the player on his right gets his cards. The high hand wins.

CLARIFICATION: Although only three rounds are dealt, this is hardly Three Card Stud. After a couple of folds, an aggressive player can have six or seven cards, easy. As you are probably aware, it still takes five cards to make a straight or a flush. As with other games where one player's fold can steal the game

from someone else, the last legal time to fold is when the action is on you. And, in this case (as with Countdown) you must actually owe money to the pot to fold.

BACKGROUND: Nothing hurts worse than having to fold a merely decent hand because some jerk kept raising and reraising, and then realizing that your cards are going to help him win. Don't play this game if you have anger management issues. Don't play this game if small insignificant things going wrong, like they *always* do, turn you into a seething ball of hate. Don't play this game if your night at the table will cause you to climb into your car at midnight, turn off the headlights, and rocket down the freeway at ninety-five miles an hour in the wrong lane with an open bottle of 151 and the stereo cranked to Metallica. Unless that's what you do when you win.

SUPERMAN

Seven Card Stud. Kings ("Superman") are wild. However, if a player has an Ace ("Kryptonite"), his Kings are low instead of wild. A Queen ("Lois Lane") can cancel the effect of an Ace, but only if the player doesn't include the Queen in his five-card hand.

VARIANTS: In some houses that play this classic, Supermen are dead, not low, with an Ace in the hand, and Lois Lane can carry it away even if she plays. We happen to prefer the cuter Lois rule, where she can save Superman as long as she doesn't get to play. No matter how you play, you can't make a King into a Queen just to carry away the Kryptonite. For one thing, the timing is all wrong, since the King isn't wild unless the Kryptonite is already out of the room. For another, that's just sick.

TAMMY WYNETTE

Seven Card Stud. If a player has a Queen in his five-card hand, his Jacks and Kings are wild. If not, his Jacks and Kings are dead. (The Queen never becomes wild or dead.)

BACKGROUND: Named for The First Lady of Country Music and her anthem *Stand By Your Man*, with a slight nod to her predictable follow-up *D-I-V-O-R-C-E*.

VARIANTS: In *Oedipus*, instead of the above rule, if any player in the showdown shows both a Jack and a Queen in the same seven-card hand, then all Kings are dead.

TANZANITE

Seven Card Stud. When players fold, they must turn their hole cards faceup. If only one Ace has been dealt, it is worth four Aces of that suit. If two Aces have been dealt, each Ace is worth three Aces. If three Aces have been dealt, each Ace is worth two Aces. If all four aces have been dealt, each is worth just an ace. Six Aces is the highest hand. (Though, technically, only five of them actually play. Like it matters.) At the showdown, all players must show their hand for a proper Ace count.

BACKGROUND: Named for the precious jewel found only in Tanzania, and not much there any more. The best thing about precious gemstones is that, the less of them you can manage to dig up, the more each one is worth. Spending precious Tanzanian resources digging up worthless rocks helps raise the value of tanzanite that was mined years ago. No kidding. Why, it's a wonder they don't just start digging everywhere like crazy people, opening expensive mining operations in Zimbabwe and Monaco, nearly guaranteeing that they won't find any more tanzanite, and driving the value of their existing stockpiles through the roof.

TEN O'CLOCK HIGH

Five Card Draw. Hands higher than a pair of 10s cannot win a showdown. If all players in the showdown have hands higher than a pair of 10s, high hand wins.

CLARIFICATION: A pair of Aces is the highest pair, so you can't call your Aces low. Also, straights and flushes destroy your hand.

STRATEGY: A game where betting like a crazy man actually indicates that you are one. You know your only hope when you get three 9s is to bet everyone out, and everyone else does too. So maybe you should do this when you have *two* 9s.

The Big Ten: 3–5–7

Bloody Sevens . . . Heinz 57 . . . 3–5–7 . . . Say their names with reverent pride. These games send a chill down the spine, and they coincidentally all have wild 7s. We can't really explain their popularity, except for the obvious reason that 7 is a lucky number, so people tend to make up games revolving around it in which it's possible to get very, very unlucky.

3–5–7 is a multi-round, multi-hand Guts-style game that usually drags on for what seems like twenty or thirty dollars. You will need three "leg" markers per player, and a button, which starts on the dealer. Even if you don't normally play with an ante, everyone must ante a nickel to start this pot. That's because there's no betting.

Start by dealing three cards to each player. In this round, 3s are wild, and you will be comparing for best three-card hand (no straights, no flushes). The player on the dealer's left goes first, declaring either that he is either "checking" or "in." The next player in sequence does the same, but once a player has gone in, players cannot check; at this point, they must declare whether they are "in" or "out." This follows around the table all the way back to the first player who was in, so that someone who checked early can still come in later. All players who are "in" compare their cards secretly, and each player pays the amount in the pot to all the players who beat them. So if there are four players in the round, there will be one winner who collects the amount from the other three, one player who pays the winner and collects from the other two, and so on. If only one player stays in the round, he earns a leg marker. A player needs at least three legs to win the pot.

Next, players receive two more cards, for a hand of five. The button moves one place to the left, and players ante another nickel. The same bidding process takes place, including players who were out of the first round, and this time only 5s are wild.

This repeats again with a third ante and hands of seven cards. In the third round, only 7s are wild. After the seven-card round, players discard their hands, the button moves again, and a new round is dealt. This repeats until one player gets his third leg, and that player has at least two more legs than anyone else. At this point that player wins, and takes the money in the pot (anticlimactic, really, compared to beating five other players for the same amount).

CLARIFICATION: For ease of play, one player (the dealer) should be in charge of handing out the legs, and another player (someone who likes being "the bank" in Monopoly) should keep track of the pot. This player should take time to swap in bigger chips to change up all those nickels, so that the pot is easier to count. Before each betting round, this player's job is to announce the amount currently in the pot.

BACKGROUND: This game is sometimes pronounced "three-fifty-seven," like the handgun, and this is probably what it's named after. Whether this is true or not, playing this game certainly feels like to having a gun to your head.

STRATEGY: There's a saying in our circle that "everyone pays $20 to learn how to play 3–5–7." There's some truth to that. Expect a lot of money to move around the table.

A medium pair is good enough to play in the three-card round, not only because it has a halfway decent chance of winning, but because it's smart to play in this round just to see the other players' cards. Hopefully by the seven-card round you will have seen a few cards from at least some hands you're fighting against. On the flip side, you might not want to show off your 5s and 7s until the rounds when they're wild.

VARIANTS: *See also* Guts *and* Legs, which have the same spirit of adventure and excitement but without the added thrill of wild cards.

California Guts: This game combines Legs and 3–5–7. It's two cards played for low, then three cards played for high with 3s wild, then four cards played for low, then five cards played for high with 5s wild, then six cards played for low, then seven cards played for high with 7s wild. Straights and flushes don't count against you for low, and of course you need five cards to make one. Hard to believe that money could change hands more often than in a game of 3–5–7, but there you are. We doubled it with no effort at all. Give us a week and we'll double it again.

THREES CALL

Seven Card Stud. If a player gets a 3 faceup, he must immediately decide whether the hand will be played for high or low. If another player gets a 3 faceup, he gets the same choice. On the last card, each player may opt to take his card faceup or facedown; there is no cost either way. If no 3s are ever dealt faceup, the hand is played for high.

BACKGROUND: A devilish game because you don't know what you should be shooting for. This bugs any number of players, who feel that they have some sort of influence over what card is dealt next, and certainly would not have wasted their energy wishing for a King if they'd known they should have been wishing for a 4. These are the kind of people who mock those who buy their lottery tickets with the number chosen by the machine, as opposed to picking them themselves. People who want the illusion that they have control over their lives should not be playing with instantly randomizable objects, we think.

THE THREE STOOGES

Five Card Draw. Before the deal, three cards are placed facedown in the center. Play Five Card Draw as usual. After the second betting round, the first center card ("Larry") is exposed, and all cards of its rank are wild. There is a round of betting. Next, the second card ("Curly") is exposed, and is a community card, i.e., all players may use it in their hands. Then there is another bet, and the third card ("Moe") is exposed. All cards of its rank are dead, including Larry and Curly, if they match. There is a final betting round, then a showdown for high hand.

VARIANTS: It's possible to add the Three Stooges to pretty much any Five Card Draw game that doesn't already have community cards. For example, we like Hamlet Meets the Three Stooges (described under Hamlet) and Frankenstein meets the Three Stooges, in which the Monster hand plays by the same rules as everyone else, but may wait to discard down to five until after the Stooges are revealed.

The Marx Brothers: Before dealing, expose one card and burn it, saying "That's Gummo." Then deal four cards facedown into the center. The first card is Groucho (wild); the next two cards are Harpo and Chico (community cards, revealed together); and the last card is Zeppo (dead). If you use either of the community cards in your hand, you have to use them both (even if one of them is dead).

TIC-TAC-TOE

Each player gets a hand of five cards. Nine cards are dealt into the center in a 3x3 box, with the cards at the corners starting faceup, but the other five cards in the middle (the cross) facedown. There's a betting round, then the downcard in the top row is exposed. Then another round, then the downcard in the right column is exposed, and so forth with the bottom, left, and center card turning over in that order. At the showdown, each player may use any combination of his downcards with any single row, column, or diagonal of the nine tic-tac-toe cards.

VARIANTS: Five downcards is a lot of cards, considering that you also have nine community cards and eight subsets of those cards to choose from. You can deal this game Omaha-style, giving players four cards but forcing them to use exactly two of them, or Hold 'Em style, where the players get only two hole cards, and must therefore make a hand from those two cards and any valid set of three on the grid.

A lot of players call this game *Bingo*, but we think that would require twenty-five center cards. Feel free to try that.

TOMMY TUTONE

Seven Card Stud. Queens are wild. The winner splits the pot with the hand that can dial the deepest into the telephone number 867–5309. For purposes of the dialing hand, 10s are treated as 0s, and Queens can be used as any number.

CLARIFICATION: You must start with the 8, then the 6, and so on. If you have 4-6-7-5-3-10-9, your straight better win high.

BACKGROUND: Based on the catchy ditty *867–5309/Jenny* by the titular rock group. Though we think the number really has seven tones, not two.

TWIN BEDS

Each player gets a hand of five cards, and two rows of five cards are dealt facedown in the center. The first card of each row is revealed, and then there's a betting round. This occurs four more times. At the showdown, each player may use any combination of his five cards and the five cards in one row or the other (but not both).

BACKGROUND: Phil thinks this game is about sex. Mike knows this game is from the '50s, when no one had sex. Well, Lucy and Ricky did, once, in one of their beds. That's how they got Little Ricky. And then they got back to viewing the sixteen inches between their tiny beds as the Berlin Wall. That's what made them Americans.

UPTOWN

Seven Card Stud. A player's first upcard, and all cards of that rank, are wild for that player. For example, if your first upcard is a 5, then 5s are wild for you.

VARIANTS: You can make the second, third, or fourth upcard determine the player's wild card. This will give you less information to go on in the early rounds, but it also prevents someone with a pair of wild cards from raising like crazy from the start.

Uptown Girls: Same rules as Uptown, but Queens are also wild.

WAVEFORM

Seven Card Stud, with the only difference being that the game is dealt down, up, down, up, down, up, down. There is a betting round after the first two cards and after every card thereafter, so this has one more betting round than normal.

BACKGROUND: Also called *Sine Wave, Square Wave, Elevator, Clarinet,* and *Manic-Depression.* We find it strange that a game that's hardly ever played has this many names. Maybe people think about calling it all the time, and then have second thoughts.

WELFARE

Seven Card Stud. After each betting round, the lowest hand showing takes a nickel from the pot.

BACKGROUND: The welfare state has lofty goals. It says that because we on Earth shall be judged by how we treat the least among us, we shall give the poor limited quantities of food stamps and cigarettes, while simultaneously handing million-dollar tax breaks to the wealthy. Hence it is through this game that we commemorate this visionary concept by tantalizing the low hand to stick around for one more round by rewarding it with far less money than is required to call any reasonably sized bet.

ZOMBIE NATION

Five Card Draw. An additional five-card hand is dealt facedown in the center. At the showdown, the player who reveals the second best hand may pick up the zombie hand, and draw to it as normal. If the player with the zombie hand wins, he takes the pot.

BACKGROUND: Named for the German electronica band whose "do-da-da-da-da-da-do-da-dum" song *Kernkraft 400* is played in every sports stadium in America. Feel free to sing it as you're dealing, if you can remember how it goes.

Chapter 4

WHO
LIKES
WHAT

We just gave you two hundred games to choose from, but you probably shouldn't play them all with everybody. In a dealer's choice environment, picking the right game is a test of your evaluation skills. You can make everyone happy if you know how to read the pace of your game, your friends, and your friends-of-friends.

WHAT, WHEN?

All of these games are playable at any dealer's choice night, but you might want to vary what you play and when. Some games are wild and woolly, while others are serious brain-crunchers. Your poker night should have a flow to it, like a multi-course dinner, or a symphony, or, um, like a hand of poker.

EARLY ROUNDS: These games are for when people first come over, when they all have a roughly equal stack of chips, and when their brains are fresh enough to handle long instructions. They might have some wild cards, or card modification, or strange betting rules. When some people don't know others at your table, these are good icebreakers. Five and Dime, Fusion, and Centipede fit this description.

Several of our friends always start the night with Seven Nice Cards. That's Seven Card Stud, only players must be nice. (The rules, should you need them, are under Call the

Kings.) If someone's going to ask whether a straight beats a flush, Seven Nice Cards is a great game for them to do it in. Less so in 3–5–7, when what people ask not only affects this hand, but the next one as well.

In early rounds, split-pot games work well because everybody wants to play, and split games give them the excuse. It's nice to take down a pot, or even half a pot, at least once before the night gets old. Games like Tommy Tutone, Pointillism, and Sonny & Share fit the bill.

Other openers capitalize on the social aspects of poker. Games that allow lots of talking and negotiation, like Auctioneer and Push, get players into the swing of things. Games like Cryogenic Freeze and High Fences, where players must make interesting choices that are apparent to all, are good here too. Games with open choices get players talking. Importantly, none of these games is likely to bankrupt a player, so by the time you're an hour in, everybody's still in the game.

MIDDLE ROUNDS: In the middle of the evening, players are starting to get settled. The new players now know who are the sharks at the table and who are the guppies. Now's the time for some serious poker games, ones that are easy to explain but tough to master. Try a hand of Double-Barrel Draw or Dakota.

Now's also a good time for games where players have incentives to bet like maniacs, such as Countdown and Suck. These games move money around the table, and often pull it out of people's pockets. People will feel rewarded for their good play in these rounds, or at least for drawing the 2 of Spades in Low Chicago.

These middle rounds are also when people start getting tired, and so breaking up the night with a few "games that aren't poker" is sometimes welcome. A round of Acey-Deucey might be popular, though if you run it up the flag-pole and get too many "*Hey, we came here to play poker*"s, you can back off and deal Anaconda. That's kind of like a compromise.

FINAL ROUNDS: The gloves come off at midnight, when no one's interested in hearing that you have a new variant of Johnny Mnemonic. We often stall the pot-matching games until late, so the what's-this-thing-called-poker players can lose their initial stakes a little at a time instead of all at once. Games like 3–5–7, Challenge, and Frankenstein are long games in which a lot of money moves around. At the end of the night, someone will be going home happy, or, you know, staying home happy if he's the host.

Sometimes, after we're done with the dealer's choice stuff, we play mini-tournaments of something we all know well, like Texas Hold 'Em, Seven Card Stud, or Omaha-8. An in-depth discussion of tournament play is beyond the scope of this book, but the basics are this: Everybody buys a certain amount of chips, say $10 worth, and that's all they have in the game. When a player loses his initial stake, he's out. To accelerate this, you can raise the minimum and maximum bets (or the blinds, in a game with blinds), doubling them every 20 minutes or so. At the end, the first place player gets half the total cash, the second place winner gets some fraction of what's left, and the third place player usually gets his buy-in back.

WHO ARE THESE PEOPLE?

We think the world is divided into two types of people: those who divide the world into two types of people, and those who don't. We're in the first group, so we've divided our friends into "Adventurers" and "Scientists." Adventurers love to strike out into the wilderness with nothing but a bowie knife, a ball of string, and a mortal fear of standing still. Scientists, conversely, like to have all the facts and know their degree of risk before they eat a bowl of cereal. We could have called these folks the "Loonies" and "Lumps," but that would've been pretty cruel . . . wait, actually, that's infinitely more descriptive. So. Our friends are Loonies and Lumps.

LOONIES: These players want to play something new every night, preferably every hand. When the dealer says, "This one's called The Rise of the Industrial Proletariat," the Loony will say, "Neat! How'zat work?" The most outrageous games in this collection are pure excitement for Loonies, games like Slaughterhouse-Five and Feathers McGraw. Any game in Chapter Three will work for the Loony, but ones that feature the words "wild," "dead," and "duck" will be irresistible.

That doesn't mean a Loony will *like* every game. Much of a Loony's fun is evaluating the game, then tossing it on the trash heap if it lacks the goods. The excitement comes from being thrown into the harsh wilderness and coming out on the other side with a full stomach, a bearskin coat, and a halfway decent idea of how to win. You've been dealt a low straight, but is that a winner with six conditional wild cards in the game? Running the wheels, you make your call, note the effects, and try to apply those lessons to the next crazy game.

The Loony's desire for a new game makes easy picking for those who already know the game. If you've played plenty of Anaconda, think back and recall what new players might expect. When you see a medium straight building in a player's hand, you'll know right away that player has misjudged the game.

For their part, Loonies gravitate toward calling certain games they know and like, because ultimately they're just as interested in winning as anyone else. They expect others to love the wilderness as much as they do, so the games will be pretty crazy. A Loony might adopt a stable of favorites like Hamlet, Countdown, and Heinz 57 because of a few basic survival skills learned specifically for those games.

LUMPS: These players just want to play something familiar. When the dealer says, "This one's called Shackleford's Polar Expedition," the Lump will say, "I'm out—Can I have a Klondike Bar?" The Lump plays an hour a day of Texas Hold 'Em online, and is using your Saturday game to "get ready for Vegas." And Vegas, as we know, doesn't run tournaments of Juncture of Destiny. If the game isn't "real poker," like the kind they deal at the Bellagio, the Lump is only playing to be polite.

These games are also the only games you'll hear this dealer call, unless peer pressure has forced him to go out on a limb and, sometime after midnight, call one hand of "High-Low Split." He probably will call a full round of Hold 'Em when he deals, ostensibly because it's more fair but really because he just wants to play a few more hands of the game for which he actually knows some charts.

But you can still mix it up with a Lump, within reason. The Lump will play Five Card Stud (they used to play that in casinos) as well as variants of Hold 'Em or Omaha, like The Strip, Courchevel, or Pineapple. The Lump will play Mississippi or Enigma, because those games teach useful decision-making skills, and might even play Guts or Legs,

because those games are far enough away from poker that confusion will be avoided while still offering the thrill of making decisions about a significant amount of money. Just like when the Lump decides whether to stay in a good casino with a poker room, or a cheap casino that leaves him money left to play.

The Lump is less comfortable when wild cards or dead cards enter the picture, and might use the term "candy-ass" to describe such a game, with a frequency proportional to the number of wild cards. A Lump won't even put a nickel into a game with a death card; why, he wonders aloud, would anyone put money into a pot if they knew there was a card that could kill their hand? (It's bad enough, he figures, when legitimate cards ruin you.) The Lump isn't trying to be rude; he just doesn't get the appeal of the crazy rollercoaster of games in this book.

MIXED LUMPS AND LOONIES: Most people don't fall on either extreme end of this scale, but they do lean one way or the other, and most groups are composed of a blend of both types. But a mix of the two extremes can put the host in a tough spot. The Lumps will bore the Loonies with their methodical play, and the Loonies will chase out the Lumps with their crazy games. If you have enough players in this situation, the best answer is to split the house into two tables, a higher-limit table for Hold 'Em or Stud and a "kids' table" where anything goes. Even with only eight players, this can sometimes be a smart thing to do.

It's also smart to tell the Loonies to cool it with the nutball games like Zombie Nation and Sonny & Share until the Lumps migrate to the couch to watch *World Series of Poker* reruns. If *Celebrity Poker* is on instead, the Loonies can drift away to watch that guy yell "Man without fear!" at Ben

Affleck, and the Lumps can finally play round after round of Omaha-8.

But really, you have a lot of friends. The best idea is to be specific about what you'll be playing when you send out your invitations. Then you can say to the Loony, "Hey, you knew we were only going to be playing H.O.R.S.E. tonight, so you can leave the egg timer and dice at home."

WAIT, YOU BROUGHT *HIM*?

We know, you like your friends. They're the ones who come to your house, play cards, lose money, eat potato chips, and go home happy. But sometimes you have to deal with those friends-of-friends who sneak past the most effective security systems, including that trusted watchdog, "Don't bring anyone I don't know to my house." Don't panic; most of them will be fine. There's just a few that require special handling. We've played with all of them, and we know a few tricks to keeping everybody happy without spilling blood. Much.

Here are eight personality types you should watch out for. They wear all kinds of disguises, so you will only know them when they act out.

MORGAN, THE NICKEL CLUTCHER: There's this guy who we'll call Morgan. Every time we call a game he hasn't heard of—say, Chicago—he clutches his nickel chip and fixes a laser-beam stare on the dealer's head. Only after he's learned every rule and each subtle nuance of the game does Morgan let the chip fall into the pot and let the deal continue. We want to say, "Morgan, it's just a nickel—lighten up and have a little faith."

If you have a Morgan in your game, you've probably

become terrified of calling a game like White Chernobyl or Rosencrantz and Guildenstern. Morgan will hold up the deal until you recite the rules very slowly, possibly more than once.

Morgan's not stupid. On the contrary, he's just smart enough to be trouble. A stupid player would just play your game and lose. But Morgan has to shine his big brain on everything before he risks 5 cents. He has to be able to understand what hands will win and how much he stands to risk. At least, he has to think he does. When you're explaining a game, you must help Morgan by lacing your explanation with strategy hints. In Low Hole Wild, you don't just say, "Last card up for 50 cents." It's, "You can buy your last card up for 50 cents, which, Morgan, you might do if, say, your low hole card is paired and you don't want it to stop being wild. See?"

If Morgan is pulling this too often, offer to buy Morgan's ante on any new game you call. This makes the game free just long enough for him to hear the rules while you deal. Just don't be too generous with this, unless you like Morgan more than you like nickels.

The best thing you can do if you have a lot of Morgans is to play dealer ante. When the dealer antes for all players, his utterance of "Low Hole Beverly Hills French Revolution with the Hope Diamond" doesn't bother anyone, or even if it does, they can't hold up the deal by clutching their nickels. When it's the dealer's money, everyone feels like he's in this crazy game for free, at least long enough to hear the rules.

BOB, THE "IS-THIS-GOOD?" GUY: In a Five Card Draw game Mike was in, a young man asked, "What does it mean when you have two of one kind and three of another?" It meant fold, fold, fold, fold, fold, gentleman takes the pot. And, as it turns out, it also meant two hearts and three spades.

That guy—we'll call him Bob—is the player who always asks what the order of hands is, despite having been told repeatedly. If he doesn't care, you think, he should stop asking. Especially at the most inconvenient time, like when you're showing most of a straight, but you've actually got a flush. The important thing is that Bob really has no idea what the hand order is, and you wish he would finally learn it or get the heck out of your house.

This does you no good. By all means, if Bob wants to keep playing at your house, don't drive him out no matter how many times he forgets that a straight beats two pair. The times he is surprised to win will be vastly outnumbered by the times he is surprised to lose.

If you actually want to help Bob, write a cheat sheet and keep it at the table. Phil's got two handwritten cheat sheets that pass around, educating new players in the order of hands and in the importance of not getting caught looking at the cheat sheet. Even better, post one on your wall. Of course, you'll still get a sickening feeling every time Bob stares at the wall, but at least his monologue will be internal.

You will confuse these players to no end when you call games where the hand order changes. For example, straights don't count in San Francisco. That's one less trouble spot for Bob, so maybe it helps, but don't count on it. A Lowball game probably won't ever venture into the straight/flush/full house Bermuda Triangle, but instead you'll have a whole new set of "opportunities" to explain exactly what qualifies for low.

JOHNNY ROUNDERS: You should see *Rounders*. It's a pretty good movie, and it has Matt Damon in it, and whether you like him or not, you should see it. In fact, even if you hate the film, you should probably watch it twice.

Here's why. There's this guy, we call him Johnny Rounders, who really likes that movie. He shows up at all the low-limit tables in Las Vegas and even creeps into people's home games from time to time. Johnny's distinguishing characteristic is his battle cry: the entire script of *Rounders*.

Johnny learned everything he knows about poker from watching this movie. From Matt Damon putting six guys on bad hands in ten seconds to John Malkovich sputtering out the indelible line "Paye dat me-yan his moneych," Johnny has absorbed all the coolness of *Rounders* and he is now here to share it with you.

Now, the dialogue in this movie isn't that bad, for a poker movie, and there isn't a world-class player alive who doesn't call Texas Hold 'Em the "Cadillac of Poker." But what's different about Johnny Rounders is that his vocabulary stops at the edges of this movie, and nothing he says about the game seems to come from anywhere else.

Johnny Rounders might use a phrase like "I flopped a straight" in a Seven Card Stud game. He might fiddle with his chips as if they were Oreos. He's got a peculiar way of saying "Jacks?" like a New York deli owner, or "Take it down" in a surreal Russian accent. He'll even say "I'm sorry, John, I don't remember," when there's no one at the table named John.

The point is this: Johnny's battle cries in all their varied but instantly recognizable forms translate to the same phrase: "Take my money!" He is that rarest and most valuable of all game animals, one who is just smart enough to lose. He is desperate to show you how sophisticated he is while simultaneously still curious what seven cards might look like. In short, Johnny Rounders is your new best single-serving friend.

Make him comfortable. Speak his language. Quote the movie back to him. Then, by God, take all his money before someone else does.

BILLY, THE KID: Lots of kids are taking up poker these days. Not surprisingly, all three of us learned this game long before we were old enough to drink and drive. We aren't qualified to raise anybody else's kids, and we're pretty sure that gambling with minors is illegal even where it's legal otherwise, so we're not going to advise anyone under 18 to play for money. Still, they're out there, and your group may eventually have to decide whether kids are going to play with you. And hey, kids can always play if it's free.

It helps to understand there's a reason "the kids' table" is called what it is. Many candyish games in here have tremendous appeal to the short-attention-span set. When we play-tested the games in Chapter Three, the person who most liked the games with crazy betting rules was a fourteen-year-old whom we'll call Billy. If you're going to play on the bleeding edge, you might find kids are well suited for those games. After all, if you've ever seen kids on BMX bikes imitating Dave Mirra, you know they know something about gambling.

What you don't know is whether Billy has yet discovered the *consequences* of gambling. So you might stake him, just to avoid teaching him that lesson on your watch. If five adult players buy in for $5, they can each add in a buck to cover the youngster's stake. When Billy's out of money, his poker-playing day has ended. When he gets older, you'll tell him, he can put his own money in.

If Billy's buying his own chips, a big-stakes games like

No-Limit Hold 'Em or 3–5–7 can eat his whole allowance in one hand. Some players might be uncomfortable taking that much money off someone of that age. For that matter, some might not be able to handle *losing* that much to someone of that age. Make sure everyone's okay with every conceivable consequence, or call these games after Billy's mom picks him up.

LINDA AND DAVE, THE FRIENDLY COUPLE: Mike's House Rules include a rule forbidding couples to sit together. This rule came from the same experience in which Mike encountered those delectable but exorbitant deli trays. In a game of 3–5–7, Mike found himself squeezed between two players who played nearly every hand as if both had royal flushes every time—even on the three-card rounds. Those two players were, surprise, husband and wife Dave and Linda, and they were colluding.

Linda and Dave start out playing normally, even getting into a few showdowns against each other. But suddenly, when the stakes matter, they fuse into the mighty LinDave, a single autonomous robot that exists solely to raise and reraise the pot when either one has a good hand. If Linda's in the pot, so's her man. If you have a hand that might beat them both, you'll be whipsawed into paying the maximum to play it.

Not all couples do this. All of our spouses play poker, and they play perfectly straight and get significant satisfaction out of beating us. But some couples do collude, as do teams of clever cheats who don't happen to be couples. Occasionally, when they're not aware of their own behavior, they give off telltale signs such as the starting-gun maxim, "Well, it's all the same money." From that point on, either one half of the robot will lay down when the other goes in, or they will always stay in together to raise the pot as high as they can. The latter, the more egregious of the two actions, is why a three-raise maximum became standard.

To stop this, you pretty much have to break the couple up, or convince them to play straight. They probably aren't beyond help, but they should be informed that their actions are screwing up the game. If you tell them they can't sit together, you're implying that you'll be making sure they don't collude in more meaningful ways.

BUDDY, THE DRUNK: At a gaming convention in Vegas, the inebriated Buddy and his equally impaired friends sat down at Mike's open table. They'd seen some poker on TV, played a little when they were kids, and wanted to get back into the game during a moment when they were at their least capable. Within a few hands, Mike cleaned the guys out and sent them on their way to clean themselves up.

Was that the right approach? It wouldn't have been if the game was at Mike's house. See, then they would have *driven* to the game. That would have put them back in their cars in Mike's neighborhood. In that case, Mike would call the slowest games he could think of, cut off their alcohol supply, and then, after at least an hour without booze, win their money and send them home in a cab.

Players like Buddy want two things: more alcohol and more fun. Sober players might not find them as much fun, though, because they play like maniacs. While this is happening, you'll watch them win great pots with terrible cards, but in the long run if you can wait them out you will win it back. Despite pretending that he does, the drunk doesn't care so much about his money. He just wants a fun time with the gang before he goes home, passes out, and dreams of being beautiful.

Really, Buddy is in no state to be gambling, and players shouldn't necessarily feel good about taking his bankroll. But let's be clear: In Las Vegas, this happens all the time. People go there specifically to play both parts in this charade, the drunk and the guy who takes his money. Casinos encourage it by hiring attractive women to wear skimpy costumes and dispense free booze. At home, you can't always avoid playing with Buddy, but you can minimize the amount of time you spend with him. Either play aggressively or wait for him to crash, then get back to the real game.

JIMMY SLEEVES, THE CHEATER: At a Hold 'Em game James was hosting, he spotted Jimmy Sleeves palming cards in and out of play. And winning eight hands in a row, which even a cheater shouldn't be stupid enough to do. So James quietly counted down the deck when it was his turn to shuffle. Sure enough, a card was missing, and suddenly it turned up on the floor. No one was in the mood to accuse Jimmy of cheating, so the game quietly broke shortly after that. Later, Jimmy was (no kidding) trying to get some action by bragging about cheating in the game. Needless to say, he was never invited back. But he probably expected that.

Jimmy was taking advantage of a critical flaw in friendly poker games: if you're cheating for nickels, there's something wrong with your head. It's so damn stupid no one even looks for it. But this guy was probably practicing his chops for a bigger game where getting caught would mean more than a quiet brush-off.

The Jimmy Sleeves of the world exist, and you should do everything you can to get them out of your game. Some people simply believe that rules are made for someone else, and that it's a sin to let a sucker keep his money. Since "nice guy" and "sucker" are sort of synonymous to these bozos, they won't even stop at cheating you out of nickels.

Not every inexplicable winning streak is the result of cheating. But if you ever suspect someone, you need to let them know. If your friendship can't survive this discussion, it's not a very solid one. James knows a magician who can't help but cheat when he plays cards, for all kinds of hilarious reasons. They are still great friends, but they don't play cards.

For more on cheaters, how they do it, and how you can catch them, read John Scarne's comprehensive work on the subject, *Scarne on Cards*.

JEFF, THE MATH GENIUS: He will ruin your game. No, we joke. We love our Jeff.

Chapter 5
STRATEGY

Volumes have been written on poker strategy. But when we started looking for strategy on dealer's choice games, we pretty much came up with nothing.

Most poker books are about one game. Or, at most, two or three. They have titles like *Seven Card Stud for Advanced Players*. That's a great topic, no doubt. But a book like that will contain precious little strategy that's applicable to a nickel pot-doubling game where your opponents can't remember the rank of hands. Poker experts don't seem to like the same kinds of games we do, so it's going to be a while before we see *Night Baseball of the Living Dead for Advanced Players*. Despite the lack of material on the subject, and our own confessed inadequacies, we offer you this chapter as a stepping-off point on your long journey to find the truth.

Poker is a game involving a great deal of both luck and skill. There's not much you can do to improve your luck, but you can improve your attitude towards winning and losing. Remember the short-run effect: You can't tell from just one game whether you're playing smart or not. Just because you win (or lose) a big pot, or have a great (or terrible) session, you're probably not the world's best (or worst) poker player. The same is true of the people you play with. It may take months to figure out who's really better than whom at your weekly poker game, and even that data isn't very good, since people come and go. And they learn.

As for improving your skill, there are two basic zones of poker strategy: math and psychology. "Math" includes all the technical stuff: figuring out odds, remembering what cards you've seen, dividing the money in the pot by the amount you need to bet. "Psychology" means understanding your opponents: their goals, their faults, their skills. But it also means understanding yourself. Why do you play poker? Is your goal really to win money? It's okay if the answer is no; a lot of people play dealer's choice just to have fun. In fact, that's the only good reason to do it. But if this is the truth for you, don't be so hard on yourself when you lose.

POKER MATH

The math in a dealer's choice game comes down to answering two basic questions:

Are my cards likely to win?

How much should I bet on them *now*?

"IS THIS GOOD?": How are you supposed to know if your hand is going to win? Well, that's supposedly a mystery until the showdown, but you should at least have a general clue in any given game what kind of hand you're shooting for. Staying in Anaconda with two pair is suicide, unless there are six more sheep at the table with you. But two pair is a pretty decent hand in Five Card Draw, and it's a monster in Five Card Stud. What's the difference?

Three main things influence the average value of a winning hand. The number of cards dealt to each player, the number of wild cards, and the number of players in the game. There are other in-game clues once the game has started, like how many people raise and re-raise on their first two cards. But they're making their in-game decisions based on what they think is a good hand for the game.

In a Five Card Draw game where a player can draw three cards, you should count each player as getting about one and a half extra cards, whether they actually draw or not. The reason you don't count the draw as a full three cards is that the player never has all eight cards to choose from at the same time. Every card a player can use will increase the rank of the winning hand by about one level, so if a pair is average best hand in a five-card game, two pair is okay in a six-card game, trips will usually win in a seven-card game, a straight is good with eight cards, and a flush is about what you would expect to win an average nine-card game.

It's obvious that the number of wild cards will increase the ranks of hands that win. To make a really rough guess at the effect of wild cards, increase the winning hand by one rank for every two wild cards in the game. For example, in a game where a pair is usually good, eight wild cards (say, 6s and 7s) will increase the expected best hand into the neighborhood of a flush.

As more players join the game, the quality of the best hand goes up as well. In a four-player game of Seven Card Stud, a pair is a decent hand. With eight players, you will feel good with trips or better. Again, and this is pretty rough, add one hand rank to the winner for every two players in the game.

Obviously these hand-ranking guidelines are not perfect. But they should give you a decent place to start. By these rules a two-handed game of Texas Hold 'Em would almost always be won with high card or a low pair, and a seven-handed game of Anaconda would always come down to a split between a 6–4 low and a high full house or better. Hey, actually, that's about right.

"IS THIS A GOOD BET?" Whether your hand is good is actually secondary to the expected value of your bet. Poker players calculate "pot odds" by dividing the amount of money in the pot by the amount it costs them to call, and comparing it to the odds of their hand being (or becoming) the best. This is often very hard to compute, especially with limited information and an imperfect grasp of other players' tactics, but it's still worth figuring out.

To calculate your pot odds, figure out how many individual cards you could get that would make your hand the winner, and divide that by the number of other cards you haven't yet seen. Then you compare this to the amount of money in the pot divided by the amount of money it costs you to call the bet. If the first calculation gets you a number equal to or higher than the second calculation, you should at least call.

A simple example: Suppose you are playing Two Card Stud, and you hold an Ace. There are five people in the hand, including you (eight players were dealt into the game, and three folded) and the bet is $1 to you. There is $12 in the pot, so you stand to win $12 for your $1, if you pair your Ace. Is this a good bet?

Assuming that you can discount the small chance that you will split the pot with another pair of Aces, you can assume that a second Ace will win you this pot. There are fifty-one cards you haven't seen, of which three are Aces, making the chance of pairing your Ace 3:48. To make this a fair bet, the pot would have to be offering you odds of 48:3, or 16:1. It's only offering 12:1, so the bet, on first blush, is no good. But wait, the Ace is the best starting card you could hold, and there are lots of people in the pot. Surely there's more to it than this.

And there is. For one thing, your single Ace may win without pairing as long as no one catches a pair, so your hand is better than just a "pair draw." For another, if you catch the Ace you may be able to make more money on the next betting round, assuming anyone bets or calls you. This piece of the puzzle is called "implied pot odds," and computes the pot odds based on money that's not yet in the pot.

In a situation like this, it's probably best to raise, not because it improves your pot odds (it cuts them, actually), but because you may drive people out who could otherwise outdraw you. Think about it: Everyone at the table might make a pair. If you don't pair your Ace, you want as few people as possible to play against your Ace.

Let's take a look at pot odds as they crop up in a dealer's choice environment. Say it's the last round of Heinz 57, and several players have matched the pot, bringing it to a total value of $7.85. (Whether you're among the pot-matchers or not doesn't really matter: once you put money in the pot, it's not yours anymore. This is a concept people have trouble accepting, but it's true.) You have three Kings, and you estimate that if you catch a fourth, you'll have about a 50% chance of winning the pot. (Your strongest opponent has a lot of 8s. Maybe four, maybe five.) You have seen four wild cards, which leaves four more wild cards and the last King to make your hand. You've seen twenty-four cards, so there are twenty-eight left unseen, of which five are good. The bet is a quarter to you. Do you have sufficient odds to call?

Of course you do. Actually, since the pot is this big, you have sufficient odds to call almost any bet. Sometimes the pot gets so big that you can call with almost no chance of winning, hoping that your opponent misreads her hand, departs to collect her lottery winnings, or drops dead from a meteor strike before the showdown. This pot is offering you 7.85:0.25, or 157:5, while your estimated odds of making the winning hand are 50% of 23:5, or 46:5. This ratio does mean that it would be a mistake to call a bet of a dollar, or to call when you fully expect the bet to be raised to a dollar. In this case the pot odds would be only 7.85:1.00, or about 40:5, less than the 46:5 that you need.

Professionals do this kind of analysis a lot, because they have a lot of practice and, in the games they play, the numbers are relatively easy. You probably won't do it on the fly, but if you're second-guessing yourself after a questionable call, you can run the numbers and see just how right you really were.

POKER PSYCHOLOGY

People think bluffing is a huge part of poker, and they're half right. It's a part of poker, but it's not huge. And in much the same way that it's impossible to do magic tricks for a cat, it's impossible to bluff people who are not paying attention to you. This includes the people playing in your dining room for nickels.

Expert poker players bluff, but not like you'd expect. They don't just do it by making big bets on terrible hands. They do it by making a small bet when a big one is appropriate. They do it by glancing at the television, or down at their chips, when their natural impulse is to stare at the flop. They light cigarettes, they stare at their cards, they raise their eyebrows, they force the veins in their neck to pulse just a little bit harder than normal. Basically, they whisper in a secret language that is only audible to other poker players.

The purpose of a bluff is to make someone make a mistake, behaving as though you have one poker hand when in fact you have a different one. If you play in a nickel-quarter dealer's choice game, your opponents are already making plenty of mistakes. Bluffing like a pro against these players isn't going to do anything but drive you crazy: the money isn't important to anyone, most people can barely figure out their hands, let alone yours, and absolutely no one has made a mental note of how hard the veins in your neck normally throb.

But psychology is still your friend at the nickel table. For one thing, you know that players will tend to stay in far more often than they should (the technical term for this behavior is "loose" play). Because of this, better hands will win and the pots they win will be bigger. The "better hands" part can be discouraging, as you will find that your medium-strength hands become worthless when everyone sticks around. But the "bigger pots" part makes up for it, since when you do hang in there with a drawing hand and hit it, you'll get paid off.

You can use psychology to "read" other players, though it might not do you much good. Most people who try to disguise their hands at all fall into the category of "bad actors." As Mike Caro describes in one example after another in *Caro's Book of Poker Tells*, bad actors use kindergarten psychology to disguise their hands, acting strong when they are weak and weak when they are strong. Some players are even easier to read, giggling like little children when their cards look good. But don't put too much stock in your perfect read of a nickel player's tells. You may have astutely put him on a good hand, but the fact is that it's only a hand he *thinks* is good. It may still be utter garbage.

As we mentioned above, part of understanding the psychology of poker is knowing your own weaknesses and understanding your own expectations. If you're a professional gambler, you probably treat poker as a business, approaching it studiously, seriously, and with the goal of making money. If you're serious about making money at nickel stakes, that's fine; but it's probably better just to try to keep your sanity and not worry too much about it.

If you're going to kick yourself for losing, don't play stupid. Unfortunately (and this is a true psychological fact), playing smart makes gambling no fun at all. So, on the flip side, if you're going to play crazy and have fun, don't kick yourself for losing.

FOLDING, EARLY AND OFTEN

Food maven Ted Allen once said, "Eat anything and everything you want, so long as it's natural. Just don't eat so damned much of it." The same logic applies to dealer's choice poker: You can call any game you want, but don't play so many damn hands.

Because the game changes every few minutes, and because you're here to have fun, there's a strong temptation to play every hand. You find yourself overcome with the need to see how the game "plays out," despite the fact that it's Fifth Street in a game with eight wild cards and you haven't even caught a pair. This might be the only game of Multiball all night, you say to yourself, so why not stay in? Let it go: *You* can always call Multiball again. Fold that terrible hand and let the rest of the players fight.

If you're dealing, don't pout when you drop out. And don't stay in just because you called the game. Just fold your hand and declare, "Ah Luuv to Deel!"

Books about serious poker say you should always play fewer hands than you do. Your imagination is always better than your cards. When in doubt, fold. When not in doubt, think again. Clearly, in dealer's choice, there's more volatility, and more players stick around because everyone plays too many hands. But that's no excuse to stick around when there's only one card that can help you.

In Chicago, it's easy to think "No one is betting like they've got the Ace. Maybe I can catch it on the last card." No, son, you can't. Just throw your cards away and play again sometime. Split-pot games are an especially bad trap to fall into, since you win *far* less money when you take half the pot than when you take the whole thing. Don't believe it? Okay, suppose the pot has four players at the showdown, and it's basically been these four guys for the whole hand. Each player has put in a total of a dollar, so there's $4.00 at stake. If you win, you spent a dollar to make four, for a profit of $3.00. If you take half the pot, your profit is only $1.00, just a third of what you'd make if you took the whole thing. This is oversimplifying but basically this means your hand needs to be *three times as good* to warrant shooting for only half of the pot.

Other people will not be as willing to fold as you are. When you're in, you need to evaluate whether your opponents have enough information to believe you when you lie to them. Some games have so many possibilities that bluffing everyone out, even with a moderately good hand, is next to impossible. Consider the difference between Texas Hold 'Em and Omaha-8. Structurally, they're pretty similar, but much better hands usually win high in Omaha-8, and there's the very real possibility of a split pot. So it's harder to run a bluff in Omaha-8, except among really tight players, because no one ever folds. Now apply that same comparison to Seven Card Stud and Brian Snoddy's Midget Porn. Who would drop out a game where midgets can stack up on top of each other? It's adorable! And Queens are wild!

If you do play as crazy as everyone else, the fluctuations in your bankroll will be as high as theirs. This could be good or bad; terrible players take down huge pots with stupid cards, but don't let them change how you play those same cards. Unless you want to join in the spilling of blood, just fold those rags and wait.

TREATING CHIPS LIKE THEY MATTER

The Gambler said, "You never count your money when you're sitting at the table." Sounds like the Gambler didn't sit at many tables. Metaphorically, it's reasonable advice. Don't become so obsessed with the money that you lose the point of the game: the fun, the gamesmanship, and the fleeting chances to make even more money. In the real world, when you're playing actual poker, you should count your money all the time. While you're at it, count everybody else's.

At a dealer's choice game, you have to know at least roughly how much money you have, so you can make sure you have enough to cover your bets. This is more important in a table stakes game, rather than an out-of-pocket game. In the latter, the money in your pocket is effectively on the table, along with the money at your house, the money in your bank account, and all the money you're ever going to earn.

At a table stakes game, you should make sure you have enough chips to play to the end of any hand. If you go all in, you're not knocked out of the game, but you do lose the chance to raise, and you also (though it seems weird to put it this way) lose the chance to fold. Good poker is about good decisions, and losing the chance to make decisions is bad for your game. Here's a better reason to always have enough chips on the table: When you hit a great hand with very little money left, you can't win nearly as much as that hand is worth.

Of course, how much money you have, on the table or in your pocket, might not matter that much when the stakes are nickels. When nickel-dime-quarter poker became popular among the GIs in World War II, a nickel actually meant something. Now, when a player says, "Oh heck, it's only a nickel," it's totally understandable. In fact, "It's only a quarter" and "It's only a dollar" are almost equally true. Really, the chips in front of you are more like points in a game than actual money. That's why you're playing games like Hamlet with them.

There are two ways to overcome your natural instinct to treat the chips as valueless. The first is to accept that for the most part, they are. When we go home to our respective wives after a night of dealer's choice poker, they will invariably ask, "Howdja do?" By that, they don't mean, "Are we going to be able to afford eggs this week?" They mean, "In relation to your starting position, how do you feel about your status at the end of the activity?" Or perhaps they mean, "Did you have fun?" and, like us, couldn't care less about a fluctuation of 100 nickels. All the authors of this book married women who don't miss five bucks, and for that we're eternally grateful.

A second way to overcome the it's-only-nickels mindset: treat the chips like they *will* have value—at midnight, when the knives come out. If you play in a house where pot-matching games happen later in the night, you will need a lot of chips when that event occurs. So crazy play in the early games not only means defeat at the time, it means you're underprepared (and may have to dig into your wallet) when the big money games happen.

When you treat your chips as a downpayment on your future play in the pot-matching games, another fun side effect happens. Because you're folding hands that aren't good, you're also resting when others are expending energy on less meaningful games. When, at the stroke of midnight, some of the other players are exhausted and you're feeling good about your play and your stack of chips, you will reign. And then when you're asked "Howdja do?" when you come home, you can hand your significant other a dozen eggs.

If you already know how to talk like a poker player, you can probably skip this chapter. But if you don't, here are a few pointers that will keep you from looking stupid for at least an hour at the poker table. After that, you're on your own.

Action: (1) To "act" means to check, bet, raise, fold, or anything else the game allows on a player's turn, so it is a player's "action" when he is required to do one of these things. (2) A game with a lot of betting and raising, or generally loose play, is said to have a lot of "action." This is basically the same as (1) but is used less specifically, as in, "There's a lot of action at Dave's Friday game."

Aggressive: Having bet or raised. The phrase "last aggressive player" refers to the person who bet or raised last on the previous betting round.

All In: Being "all in" means all of a player's chips are in the pot. In a table stakes game, a player is not allowed to buy more chips during a hand. Rather than being eliminated, the player is cut off from winning any of the money from subsequent bets. This is accomplished by creating a side pot for which the all-in player cannot compete.

Ante: From the Latin for "before," the money put in the pot before the game begins. This is usually a small amount from each player, though in some houses it is posted entirely by the dealer.

Bad Beat: A very good hand that gets beaten by an even better one. Players will claim to have had plenty of "bad beats" when they just played stupidly (encourage them to tell you more stories; it's nice to know how stupid people are). Many casinos actually reward players for losing with good enough hands. For example, at the Sahara in Las Vegas, a player who loses with Aces full or better takes half a prize of about $8,000. The winner of the hand takes a quarter of that prize, and the remainder of players at the table split the rest. However, as James can tell you from experience, there's no prize for *tying* with Aces full. Of 7s.

Bank: Also called the house, the person (in home games, usually a player) who is responsible for distributing chips and keeping track of the cash. His responsibilities include accurately counting money, correctly stacking chips, and credibly pretending that the chips aren't worth far less (or far more) than the money that bought them.

Bet: To put money into the pot that must be matched by the other players. Not all money you put into a pot must be matched. For example, buying an extra card is not a bet.

Betting Round: A sequence of bets, or opportunities to bet. The round moves around the table to the left, and ends when all bets are called or when all but one player folds.

Blaze: Any five face cards, an obsolete poker hand that used to outrank a flush.

Blind: A forced bet made before the cards are dealt. In casino games like Texas Hold 'Em, a blind bet is used to start the pot instead of (or in addition to) an ante. There's often a small blind and a big one. Blinds are typically not used in a dealer's choice game, though they can be added for a full round of a game like Hold 'Em.

Bluff: (1) An ancient predecessor of poker played in the 1800s, where only the cards from 10 to Ace were used, and straights and flushes hadn't even been thought of yet. (2) To act like you have better cards than you do. A dangerous activity in games where everyone can and probably does have a great hand, or when no one's paying attention to you. In "real" poker, there's also a thing called a semi-bluff, which is a bet with a hand that's no good right now (say, four to a straight), but that might still improve and win if your opponent doesn't drop out.

Board: All one player's upcards. In a community card game, all the community cards.

Boat: A full house, derived from "full boat," which means, uh, "full house."

Bobtail: A four-flush or open-ended four-straight. A little bobtail is three cards to a straight or flush, and a big bobtail is four cards to a straight flush. These aren't real hands, but old timers like to use phrases like this when they're telling bad-beat stories.

Both Ways: When a player declares that he will win both halves of a split pot, declared by a player typically going for both high and low hand. It could also be both the all-red and all-black hand, the high hand and the best Blackjack hand, or whatever the game demands. Usually, if a player doing so doesn't win both, he wins nothing.

Bring-In: A minimum bet that starts the first betting round. Sometimes a particular hand must bring it in. For example, in casino-style Seven Card Stud, the low card on the deal must bring it in (bet first) for at least the table minimum bet.

Bullet: An Ace. Part of the quaint Oldie-Westie sequence of names for high cards, including Cowboy (King), Lady (Queen), and Jake (Jack). See, Bullets are the only things that take out Cowboys....

Burn: To take a card out of play, usually without showing it. Cards are burned before the deal in Texas Hold 'Em because of the possibility that one player can read a mark on the top card of the deck. Knowing the next card helps so much that it pays to get rid of that card and deal the card that follows, after all the betting is done.

Busted: Not complete. When you draw to a big hand and don't hit it, you have a busted hand. For example, in Five Card Stud, A–K–Q–J–8 is a "busted straight."

Button: An oversized chip, decorative card box, or mummified monkey hand representing the position of "dealer," useful in any game where it's necessary to change who acts first. In a game with multiple rounds, the button passes around the table so that the action is not permanently on the player to the real dealer's left.

Call: To put the same amount of money as the previous bettor into the pot.

Cards Speak: A fairly universal rule that, in the showdown, if you mis-call your hand, your cards (i.e., the other players) can tell you what you really have. In a crazy game with multiple conditional wilds like Girl's Best Friend, a cards-speak rule means that if you declare that you have a straight but you actually have a full house, you aren't required to stick with the straight.

Case: The "case card" is the last remaining card of a particular rank. For example, if three of the 9s have been accounted for, the last one is the "case" 9. According to Scarne, this term comes from the game of Faro, in which the entire deck was dealt from a solid case, and it was theoretically important to know when there was only one of a card left, or "cased."

Cash Out: To return your chips to the bank for an equivalent amount of cash upon leaving. Distinguished from "cash it in," which also involves leaving but may not involve cash.

Catch: To get a card necessary to complete a hand. For example, if you have four to a flush, you might "catch" the fifth card on the next round.

Chase: To draw to a higher hand, trying to "catch." If you understand math, it's easy to figure out when the odds justify chasing a particular hand, and when they don't. If you're fuzzy on the math, just do what your mother told you and never draw to an inside straight.

Check: (1) To bet nothing. (2) What you will have to write somebody after a game of Frankenstein.

Check-Raise: Raise the bet after having checked on the same betting round. (In other words, you check, someone bets, and then you raise.) Check-raising is considered impolite by some players, but is also considered a critical element of professional poker. Your house rules should specify whether check-raising is allowed.

Coffeehouse: To talk about one's cards during a hand, or play-act or kibitz to distract other players. Discouraged in some games, encouraged in Johnny Mnemonic.

Community Card: A card in the center of the table that is shared among players' hands. Also sometimes called a spit card (after the game Spit in the Ocean).

Connectors: Cards that are next to each other in rank, such as 7–8. "Suited" connectors are cards of the same suit and next to each other in rank.

Cut: To take some of the cards off the top of a deck and move them to the bottom. When cutting for the dealer, it's polite to cut the top half of the pack towards the dealer and then let the dealer complete the cut.

Dead Card: A card that is not considered to be in the game at all. Note that this is different from a low card, q.v.

Dead Man's Hand: Two pair, Aces and 8s. There's some debate about exactly which Aces and 8s they were; we think it was the black Aces, black 8s, and the 9 of Diamonds, but it's certainly named after the hand of cards that Wild Bill Hickok was holding when some angry buck shot him in the brainpan.

Dealer: The person dealing the cards. It's often required to designate another "dealer" with a button, since the same player may deal several rounds of the same game while the button, and with it the nominal role of dealer, passes around the table.

Dealer Ante: An ante structure where the dealer pays the whole ante, equal to a small amount per player. Useful in a dealer's choice game, to allow players to fold without cost when they are dealt a game they would never, ever pay to play.

Dealer's Choice: A version of poker in which the deal passes each game and each dealer can choose, or invent, a new poker game each hand.

Death Card: A death card is a card that, if you have it, means you can't win the hand. Death cards are critical elements in some of the stupidest and deadliest games, such as Good Cop, Bad Cop and Bloody Sevens.

Declaration Round: A time after the last betting round of a split-pot game when players declare whether they're going high, low, or both ways. It usually involves players concealing chips in their hands. Your house rules should specify the method of declaration, such as "Zero for low, one for high, and two for both ways."

Deuce: According to the *Professional Poker Dealer's Handbook*, there are no 2s and 3s in poker, just Deuces and Treys. We think that's a bit extreme, but if you're confused, Deuce means 2 and Trey means 3.

Discard: To put a card from your hand facedown into a pile, typically in a draw game. Sometimes the discards return to life in Earth-shattering ways; see Frankenstein for one such game.

Dog: (1) A hand that is not favored to win, often shortened from "underdog," as in the phrase "2-to-1 underdog." (2) The big dog or little dog, which chase the cats. See the game Cats and Dogs for how to rank these hands.

Door Card: A player's first upcard in a game like Seven Card Stud.

Downcard: A facedown card.

KNOWN PRIMARILY FOR HIS 1876 'DEADMANS HAND', WILD BILL HICKCOCK ACTUALLY INVENTED A NUMBER OF UNUSUAL POKER HANDS...

APRIL 6TH, 1874
3♥·7♥·7♣·8♥·J♣

DECEMBER 6TH, 1874
4♣·6♣·8♣·Q♣·Q♦

SEPTEMBER 12, 1875
3♦·3♠·3♥·J♣·A♠

MAY 3rd, 1876
10♥·J♥·Q♥·K♥·A♦

©P.Faglio-04

Drag Light: To pull chips from the pot to indicate that you don't have enough money to cover your bet. In a non–table-stakes environment, this is a permissible way to track the money you owe to the current pot. This amount will come from your pocket if you lose.

Draw: (1) To take cards in a drawing game, such as Five Card Draw. (2) A hand that is not yet complete, also called a "drawing hand." For example, four clubs is a "flush draw" as long as there are cards to come. To "draw out" on someone means to get cards (often improbably) that make your hand better then theirs.

Drawing Dead: Taking cards when it is mathematically impossible to win. Usually, when you're drawing dead, you don't know it. This is either because the winner's hand is smartly concealed, or you're too stupid to figure it out. A hint for actual players we've met: In Low Hole Wild, if a player is showing four cards to a flush, he has a flush.

Drop: In Guts or other such games, to hold cards a few inches above the table and drop them if you want to be out. Otherwise you're in, so pay attention.

Duck: (1) A Deuce. (2) A critical requirement in the game of Duck Konundrum.

Edge: A valueless coin awarded to the player who won the hand, replacing his ante in the next game. This item is unique to Phil's house, and serves only as a distraction and to reduce the pot value (slightly) in a pot-doubling game. We stole the term from a 1994 card game called *Jyhad*, but it turns out that "edge" is an obsolete term for ante.

Exchange: To discard one card and receive another.

Expose: To turn a downcard faceup.

Face Card: A Jack, Queen, or King. Face cards are also called "picture cards," or "paint." Aces aren't face cards, no matter how much your little brother whines.

Fill: To get a card that completes a hand, such as a straight. Typically used to describe catching a card in the middle of a straight, though "filling up" is oddly reserved for converting two pair into a full house.

Fish: Inexperienced players. The kind of soft, delicious players that bring old professionals out of retirement when cable television brings poker back into style.

Five of a Kind: Five cards of the same rank, the best possible hand and only possible with wild or modified cards.

Flash: To accidentally show cards during the shuffle or deal. Some people will tell you you're doing it. Some people won't. Do it once in a while on purpose to learn who your friends are.

Flop: In Hold 'Em, Omaha, and similar games, the first three community cards, dealt at the same time. The word can also be used as a verb, as in "I flopped the nuts." Expert players regularly utter this phrase with no hint of irony.

Flush: Five cards of one suit, ranking above a straight and below a full house. Ties between flushes are broken by the ranks of cards in the flush, not by suit order. So any A–K–10–5–2 flush would beat any A–K–10–4–3 flush.

Fold: To drop out of a hand.

Four of a Kind: Four cards of the same rank, ranking above a full house and below a straight flush.

Hand: (1) One game of poker, from shuffle to showdown. Some variants, such as Diablo and Legs, often require multiple hands. (2) One player's cards.

Heads Up: When a game has only two players, it is "heads up." In houses with a limit on raises, that limit is often ignored when the round is heads up, meaning technically that when only two players were in at the start of the betting round, they can raise each other indefinitely.

High Card: (1) The highest card in rank, usually an Ace. (2) A hand ranked below a pair, containing no cards matching in rank or straights or flushes.

High-Low: A split-pot game where the player with the highest hand splits the pot with the player with the lowest hand. Whether the same player can qualify for both halves of the pot will depend on the game and the house rules. Such games often call for a declaration round before the showdown.

Hole: A player's down cards, especially in Stud games. "Low Hole Wild" means each player's lowest hole card (his lowest card facedown) is wild.

H.O.R.S.E.: A structured format in which the game switches between

Hold 'Em, Omaha, Razz, Seven Card Stud, and Omaha Eight or Better, usually with a full round of each game being dealt. "Razz" is Seven Card Stud Lowball. Even though we list Razz under the name Lowball, we're not gonna change this abbreviation to H.O.L.E.S.

House Rule: (1) A rule added by the dealer to make a game more interesting, more likable, more ornery, or more fair. (2) A rule about a host's house, like "Couples can't sit next to each other" or "Bring your own beer."

Imbalanced Game: A dealer's choice game in which it is possible that players will contribute unequal amounts to the pot, such as Heinz 57, where some players can be forced to match the pot in order to continue. In such a game, computing side pots can be difficult or impossible, so these games can't easily be played for table stakes.

In: Not out. That is to say, still active in this hand. A useful distinction in a game like Frankenstein, where "in" is short for "in danger of losing a lot of money."

Inside Straight: Also called a "gutshot," a four-to-a-straight hand where the missing card is between two of the others, such as 5–6–8–9. Only one rank of card will complete this straight. An "outside" straight can have either end filled, so is usually twice as likely to improve. Some double-inside straights have the same likelihood of being filled as a normal outside straight, such as 7–8–10–J–Q–A. This hand requires either a 9 or a King to finish, and so has the same odds as a normal outside straight.

Jumping on the Grenade: (1) Calling a bet to "keep someone honest." (2) In a game like Push, taking a card just so that another player doesn't get it. As the name implies, it's not exactly in your own best interest to jump on a grenade.

Keeping Someone Honest: Calling a player who you suspect has a better hand, ostensibly with the intent of revealing a possible bluff. Players often "keep people honest" when they suspect a bluff, but typically this phrase is code for "I don't want to keep my money any longer."

Kicker: A card not crucial to a hand, used to break ties between two otherwise identical hands. For example, two Aces with a King kicker beats two Aces with a 5 kicker.

Kids' Table: A table that is playing for nickels. Used in contrast with the "grownups' table" playing No-Limit Texas Hold 'Em five feet away. The distinction is clearly meant to imply that the kids are having more fun.

Kill: (1) To declare a hand or card dead. (2) An affectation (or infection) in casino games that doubles the stakes when a player wins twice in a row.

Kitty: (1) A legally questionable cash or chip fund, collected by the house to pay for drinks, etc. (2) A central hand played by a nonexistent player, such as the Monster hand in Frankenstein.

Knock: (1) To rap the table, meaning you check. (2) In the game of Knock, to declare your hand ready for the showdown.

Laydown: A tough choice to fold a good hand. A player "lays down" his hand when he believes he is beaten, using whatever non-obvious poker clues he might have picked up during the course of play. Of course, it's also legitimate to lay down a terrible hand, but you don't usually point it out.

Leg: The markers in Legs and other games indicating that a player has won a single hand. Originally based on the concept of having to win twice (hence, two legs), the requirement in this book is that a player must have at least three legs, and at least two more than any other player, to win the game.

Limit: The minimum or maximum amount of a bet. For example, in a nickel-quarter game, the limits are 5 cents and 25 cents, representing the smallest and largest bet (or raise).

Limp In: To call a small bet, either when one believes one has a weak or drawing hand, or when one wants others to believe it.

Live Bet: A bet, usually a blind bet, which a player can raise even if no one has raised him. For example, if a player posts a live blind of $4 and is only called, he can still raise when the action comes to him.

Live Player: A player still in the hand. Notable in games like High Fences, in which players who are not alive have no chance to win, despite the implications of the rules.

Loose: Playing a lot of hands, raising and calling when a more prudent player would not. By contrast, a tight player is one who plays very few and very good hands.

Low: (1) The lowest card in your hand (as in Low Hole Wild); Aces are always high for this purpose. (2) The lowest or worst possible hand.

Lowball: A game where the lowest hand wins. There are several ways to define the low hand, some more appropriate in some games (see Chapter Two). The default definition of low should be specified in your house rules.

Low Card: (1) The lowest card by rank, usually Deuce or Ace. (2) When a card is declared "low," it is still a card, but is lower than all others and can't be used in straights. This is not the same as "dead." Thus, in Hamlet, Jacks are low. A pair of Deuces beats a pair of Jacks, and Jacks can't be used in straights. But four Jacks is still four of a kind, so don't knock it.

Match the Pot: To put in the pot an amount equal to the pot. For example, if the pot contains $1.50, matching the pot costs $1.50. Pot-matching games like 3–5–7 are sometimes called "midnight games," because in houses like Mike's, they're only allowed after midnight.

Misdeal: A deal which is ruined for some reason, and must be redealt.

Muck: To toss your cards into the middle of the table; also, the name for the discard pile.

Mustache: A King of Clubs, Diamonds, or Spades. So named because, unlike the King of Hearts, these Kings have mustaches. The mustaches are occasionally called wild.

Natural Card: A card that isn't wild or otherwise modified by the game rules. In some houses, a natural hand beats an equivalent hand that uses wild cards, though this is not generally the case.

No-Limit: A betting structure where players may wager as much as they like. Usually played table stakes, so that it's impossible to bet more than you have. But hey. You wanna play no-limit out of pocket, we're not gonna stop you.

Nuts: The best possible hand given the cards that are known. This term has the most utility in games like Texas Hold 'Em, in which common cards dictate the possible hands. You can also figure the nuts in Stud by remembering all the upcards, but it's a lot more work.

Offsuit: Not the same suit. Cards of the same suit are "suited"; do not say "onsuit."

On Tilt: Playing uncharacteristically poorly, especially after a bad beat. So named because a player on tilt might as well have a big red "TILT" sign on his forehead.

One-Eyed Jacks: The Jacks of Hearts and Spades, often declared wild. Traditionally depicted in profile, the one-eyed Jacks are the same suits in all standard decks. Be careful calling them wild with a nonstandard deck. If you must play Rescue 911 with a Harley-Davidson deck, just remember they're the last two suits alphabetically. There's also a one-eyed King, of Diamonds, called *the man with the ax* because it rhymes with *one-eyed Jacks*. Oh, and because he has an ax.

Open: To make the first bet on any betting round, sometimes afer satisfying a minimum requirement. In Jacks or Better, for example, you must hold a pair of Jacks or better to open.

Option: An optional effect, such as being able to take a downcard faceup to preserve a good Low Hole Wild hand. As with anything else, options usually cost money.

Out of Pocket: The opposite of table stakes. In an out-of-pocket game, players may add more money to the table in the middle of a hand, thus being allowed to risk all the money they have in the world, and all the money they will ever have, on every hand. This is terrible in a big-money game with strangers, but perfectly acceptable in a nickel game with your friends.

Out of Turn: When it is not one's turn to act. Acting out of turn is bad manners, since it gives more information to players who have yet to act in turn.

Outs: Cards that would significantly improve a hand, ostensibly to the point where it would win. A player holding 5–6–7–8 has eight outs (four 4s and four 9s) to make a straight. Twelve other cards (the remaining 5s, 6s, 7s, and 8s) would improve his hand to a pair, but they aren't likely to make it the winner. A player with two pair, who needs a full house to win, has just four outs.

Over the Top: Reraising. Used in the phrase, "That feller came over the top and reraised me $10,000."

Pair: Two cards of the same rank, such as a pair of 9s. This hand beats high card, but loses to two pair.

Pass: (1) To check. (2) To fold. If you say "pass" in a big money game, be sure people know which definition you are using. (3) To hand cards to another player, as in Anaconda.

Pat Hand: A hand in five-card draw that drawing won't improve; for example, a straight. "Standing pat" means drawing no cards.

Pay the Pot: To pay another player the amount in the pot. This is different than matching the pot, in which the money goes into the pot. In this case, the amount goes straight to the other player.

Penny-Ante: Literally, an ante of a penny. Not done so much any more except at the kid's table. The one with real kids.

Player Ante: An ante structure where each player puts in a small bet before each game. As distinct from dealer ante, where the dealer antes for all players.

Pocket Pair: A pair concealed in one's downcards. A pair of Aces is sometimes called "Pocket Rockets." Make of that what you will.

Positional Advantage: A flaw in many poker games where a specific seat has the best (or worst) odds at the table. In some games this advantage is nearly zero; in others, it is so strong that it's a good idea to change the rules. Positional advantage is nullified if a group plays the same game all the way around the table, as is done in games like Hold 'Em, but in a dealer's choice environment this is rarely done.

Post: To bet, usually before the game begins. "Posting" almost always refers to an ante or a blind bet. In other table games, such as Blackjack, "past-posting" means cheating by adding more money to your bet after you see your cards. If you want to past-post in poker, sneak an extra bet into the pot while no one is looking. Actually, no one will stop you.

Pot: The money in the center, which will go to the winner(s) of the game.

Pot Limit: A structure where the maximum bet or raise is equal to the amount in the pot. It pretends to be less brutal than no-limit, but no one's buying that.

The Power: An aggressive player, or one with the best upcards. The statement "I check to the power" is often used to describe one's action when the most aggressive player is not the person with the best hand showing.

Protect: To put some object, perhaps a colorful chip, amusing glass frog, or angry hedgehog, on your cards so they don't get discarded by mistake. This is most useful in a game like Hold 'Em, where it's easy for the dealer to mistake your hand for a discard.

Puppy Feet: Clubs. They look like little puppy feet. No, really, they do. Call them puppy feet in a cardroom and get treated to thirty minutes of free poker advice.

Put On: To "put someone on a hand" is to guess his hand. It's important to start with a good guess and continue improving it for the duration of the game, if you can. If someone says "I put you on a flush" when you only have a pair of 9s, you have succeeded in fooling him. Even if you weren't trying.

Rags: Bad cards or meaningless low cards.

Rainbow: All four suits represented in one hand. Yes, two black shapes and two red shapes is not all that rainbowy, but that's the term. What's worse, in Hold 'Em a rainbow flop only has three suits. This term is meant to describe a situation in which there will be no flush, though a player with two suited cards could still foolishly hang around and catch two more.

Raise: To raise the amount of the existing bet. In casinos and some home games, the raise you make must be at least as large as the last bet or raise. In others, it can always vary between the minimum and maximum bets.

Rake: To take a percentage of every pot for a beer fund or some other scam, such as financing a legally sanctioned cardroom.

Rank: (1) The numeric or letter value of a card. Cards of the same numerical value or face value are said to be of the same rank. (2) The relative value of different poker hands. For example, a straight outranks two pair.

Re-Ante: To put another ante into the pot, usually before a redeal.

Rebuy: An amount of chips purchased after the buy-in. In table stakes games this can be quite structured, but in most dealer's choice sessions, a rebuy can be any amount.

Redeal: To deal a hand again, either because the rules require it or because of a misdeal.

Reraise: To raise a raise. A three-raise limit means you can only reraise twice. Or re-reraise once. Heck, it ought to just be "no re-re-reraise" for clarity.

Riffle Shuffle: A preferred method of shuffling in which the dealer splits the pack into two halves and riffles them together. Several times. Please learn how to do this if you don't know already.

River: The last card dealt in Seven Card Stud, Texas Hold 'Em, and any other game where there is such a thing as a last card dealt. Derived, probably, from the habit of naming cards after streets. In small towns. With rivers.

Rock: A very tight player. Said disparagingly by those who are not rocks.

Roll: To turn up a downcard. Used in the context of games like Roll Your Own, where you turn up one or more of your downcards.

Rolled Up: Trips on one's first three cards.

Rube Goldberg Call: A call with so many change-making motions that it's impossible to tell how much money has entered or left the pot. After sufficient flummery, the dealer is advised to count what's in the pot. And his own fingers and toes.

Runner: Two perfect cards in the last two rounds, filling an impossible hand. For example, if you have three spades after the flop in Hold 'Em, you will need two running spades to make a flush. This is also called a backdoor fill or backdoor draw.

Sandbagging: (1) Slow-playing. (2) Squeezing.

Scare Card: A card that makes another player have more respect for your hand. For example, if you bet strongly on the first round and then catch an Ace, your opponent may take it to mean that you've paired an Ace. Catching two more Aces will scare him even more.

Set: Three of a kind, often so described if it comes on the first three cards.

Show: To turn up your cards, either on cue or when you're not supposed to.

Showdown: The end of the game, in which players show their hands. Not all games make it to the showdown, but the general idea is that if you make it that far, you'll want to have the best hand.

Shuffle: To mix the cards, preferably by a riffle shuffle. Professional dealers begin with a "scramble," in which the cards are just mixed around in big lazy circles on the table. This looks childish, but is in fact the most efficient way to shuffle the cards.

Side Pot: A second pot that cannot be won by one or more players who are all-in for the main pot. In a table stakes game, when one player has gone all in, the others may continue betting into a side pot.

Skip Straight: A series of five cards separated by two steps each, such as 4–6–8–10–Q. This is an obsolete poker hand that once outranked three of a kind.

Slow-Playing: Betting very lightly or not at all with a very good hand, in the hopes of keeping other players involved and perhaps letting them catch decent hands of their own. Also called sandbagging.

Splash the Pot: To throw one's chips in the pot so that it's difficult to tell how much one has bet. This is considered bad form, mostly because there's no easy way to verify that you've put in what you said you did.

Split: (1) To share the pot. (2) What you might do to openers (in Jacks or Better) if breaking them up helps you. When you split openers you must lay your cards down by your hand and reveal them at the showdown.

Spread: (1) The range between a table's minimum and maximum bets, such as 4–8. (2) To offer a game of cards. For example, "At Charlie's Bar they spread a 4–8 Omaha-8 game with double-overs and a half kill."

Squeezing: Whipsawing between two raisers, also called sandbagging. The potential for two players to squeeze a third is the reason to impose a three-raise limit, and it explains why that limit doesn't matter when the game is down to two players.

Stack: A player's chips, whether stacked or not.

Stake: The total amount of money you have to gamble with. This can refer to your table stake (the money on the table) or to your entire gambling budget. For casual players, this is usually the same amount.

Straight: A set of five consecutively ranked cards not of the same suit, ranking above three of a kind and below a flush. An Ace can be used as high or low in a straight, so the highest straight is 10–J–Q–K–A.

Straight Flush: A straight which is also a flush, ranking above four of a kind but below five of a kind. The highest of these, 10–J–Q–K–A, is called a royal flush, but it's really just a very good straight flush.

Street: Third Street, Fourth Street, and so on are the names of the cards (and the associated betting rounds) in Five, Six, or Seven Card Stud. The last round is called the river. The river term has migrated to Hold 'Em, despite the absence of streets. If you think that's bizarre, go look at "case."

String Bet: To call, then raise in a second motion. Not accepted in professional houses and not too smart in home games, either.

Stud: A game where a player receives some down cards and some upcards, with betting rounds in between.

Suicide King: The King of Hearts, who is traditionally depicted with a sword held behind his head. Or jabbing into the side of his head, you can't really tell.

Suit Order: A rule that determines which card or hand is better by the suit. From lowest to highest (and in alphabetical order), the suits are clubs, diamonds, hearts, and spades. Suit order is used in casinos to determine which low card must open the first betting round in Seven Card Stud, but in general there is no suit order in poker.

Table Stakes: A house rule that says players can only bet with the money they have on the table. When players are all-in, meaning their chips are all in the pot, a side pot starts without them, but they are not taken out of the game. This structure is almost universal in casino games but breaks down in any imbalanced dealer's choice game where players contribute unequal amounts to the pot. Read the Table Stakes section in Chapter Two for information and alternatives.

Tell: An action or mannerism that gives away some aspect of a player's hand, like suddenly being less talkative when a good hand shows up. Players in nickel games don't have many reliable tells, because they rarely care enough about the money to let it show on their faces. For an exceptional book on the tells of professional players, read *Caro's Book of Poker Tells*, by Mike Caro.

"That's Why They Call It Poker": A meaningless mantra uttered after a bad beat, or really, after any beat. Apparently, phrases like "I'm stupid" and "that's some terrible card play on your part" aren't catchy enough. Yet somehow this one is very catchy, despite the facts that (1) it's not even a clever pun, and (2) actually, there's a lot of disagreement on the origin of the word "poker."

Three of a Kind: Three cards of the same rank, a hand that outranks two pair and loses to a straight.

Trap: A psychological ploy that gets a player to make errors, usually to put more money into a game than is prudent. Expert poker players are often so clever that they trap themselves. Inexpert poker players can live without any fear of this.

Trips: Three of a kind. *Quads* is four of a kind. This word sounds a lot weirder than Trips, probably because you get to say it a lot less. People never say *Quints*, because it sounds stupid. But it probably means five of a kind.

Turn: (1) One player's action in a betting round. (2) The fourth community card in games like Texas Hold 'Em and Omaha.

Twist: An exchanged card, also known as a substitution.

Two Pair: Two unrelated pairs of cards, such as K–K–9–9, a hand which ranks below three of a kind and above one pair.

Under the Gun: Being first to act on the betting round.

Upcard: A faceup card.

Variant: A dealer's choice game with one or more rules added or changed. Also pronounced, "Why you bought this book."

The Wheel: The lowest possible hand by the most popular definition: A–2–3–4–5. The wheel also happens to be a straight, a not-too-shabby high hand. It's also called the bicycle, apparently first by the folks at Bicycle. This is probably how it eventually came to be known as the wheel. Or perhaps it's the wheel because it goes up and down. But then, why not "the hemline?" Or "the economy?"

Wild: A wild card can become any card. In "cards speak" games, wild cards become whatever is the best possible card for the player's hand, even if the player is not smart enough to figure that out. (Read Girl's Best Friend before you roll your eyes at that.) Some houses disallow using the wild card for any card you already have, which makes it impossible to make five of a kind.

Wraparound Straight: A variant straight that wraps around the ends of the deck. A wraparound straight is ranked by its last card, so under this rule a Q–K–A–2–3 is a 3-high straight. All wraparound straights lose to all regular straights.

WSoP: Acronym (rhyming with "sys-op") of the World Series of Poker, a high-stakes poker championship shown every few seconds on ESPN. Not to be confused with The World Poker Tour, The World Poker Showdown, and the like. Good TV all around.

BIBLIOGRAPHY

The Professional Poker Dealer's Handbook (Dan Paymar, Donna Harris, and Mason Malmuth, Two Plus Two Publishing): If you think this book gets picky about rules, you ain't seen nothin'. The *Professional Poker Dealer's Handbook* is the definitive textbook for dealers. It covers the rules for every conceivable circumstance, including what to tell a player when he tries to reraise when another player's all-in raise is less than half the allowable raise. (Hint: It starts with "I'm sorry.")

Scarne on Cards (John Scarne, Signet): The definitive work on cheating, card playing, and gambling circa 1949 (revised in 1965). Scarne was a professional magician before becoming the army's foremost card shark, traveling the globe and teaching our boys how to spot cheaters. Scarne's pre-Thorpe analysis of blackjack is hamfisted and his historical reckoning is hilarious, but his method for cheating at pinochle is probably still unparalleled. His dealer's choice poker section includes such classics as Pig in the Poke, Lame Brain Pete, and Double-Barrel Shotgun.

Bicycle Official Rules of Card Games (United States Playing Card Company): As official as it gets.

www.planetpoker.com's poker dictionary (Michael Wiesenberg): This website's poker dictionary is unbelievably thorough. If you want to know what Georgia hoops or scootermockins are, head to planetpoker.

Caro's Book of Poker Tells (Mike Caro, Cardoza). Also published as *The Body Language of Poker*, this is a darned fine handbook of the many ways that otherwise clever people behave when they are playing cards for money. You can use the information in this book to put big moves over on unsuspecting career players in Vegas. But it'll do you next to no good in a home game where the biggest bet is a quarter and your opponent is too busy trying to figure out his own hand.

ACKNOWLEDGMENTS

After reading this book, you will be tempted to say, "Man, you guys need help." How true that is. We had a lot of help putting this book together, and those people deserve to see their names in print.

First up are our wives Carol, Kaja, and Evon, without whom et cetera et cetera. Our non-wifely proofreaders—Nathan Clarenburg, Andy Collins, Rick Fish, Jeffrey Louis Harris, Rei Nakazawa, and Jonathan Nowitz—reminded us which hand is the left one and that casinos really do sue those who slander them. We also share a lovely crop of friends on whom we regularly guinea-pig games, and we thank them for their incomprehensible tolerance, creativity, and losing streaks.

The fine folks at The Overlook Press showed rambunctious enthusiasm for the project. That's because our editor, David Mulrooney, is an avid poker player, and someone who can sit at our table any day. Our agent, Shawna McCarthy, cannot, because she would just stare us into giving her all our money. Thanks to both of them for making a humble little dream into a humble little reality.

All the games in this book had inventors, and it just kills us that we can't pad our word count with all of their names. About half are "public domain" games, those that have been floating around card rooms in various incarnations for years, and this means we have no idea who invented them.

The other half were invented by us, or by our gaming geek pals. This group includes E. Michael Blake (*Socialism),* E. Jordan Bojar (*Frankenstein*), Greg Collins (*Lincoln*), Frank DiLorenzo (*California Guts*), Falko Goettsch (*House of Commons, Johnny Mnemonic, Louvre,* and *Welfare*), Dan Katz (*Duck Konundrum*), The Keep Household (*Centipede* and *Foundation*), Greg King (*Two-Thirds* and *Follow Mariah*), Andrew Lockwood (*The Ring*), Rick Loomis (*Call the Kings, Push-Pull,* and *Threes Call*), Elizabeth Marshall (*Juncture of Destiny*), Carol Monahan (*Girl's Best Friend* and *Philsbane*), Rei Nakazawa (*Baby Seals* and *Tommy Tutone*), Aaron Nelson (*Jump Start* and *Mission Creep*), The Philadelphian (*Acey-Deucey with Wide Goal Posts* and *Good Cop, Bad Cop*), Marshall Simpson ("all red cards wild"), Brian Snöddy (*Brian Snöddy's Midget Porn*), Dina Varacelli (*Fool's Paradise*), Jeff Vogel (*Blow Chicago, Heinz Fixed-y Seven, Jane Austen,* and *Multiball*), and Warren Wyman (*Avocado* and *Redball*). Many thanks, guys.

And if you, dear reader, believe in your heart of hearts that you're the supergenius who came up with the Extra Innings rule for Baseball, well, many thanks to you as well. But no check.

INDEX

Games in **boldface** have their own entries. Games in *italics* are variants or alternate names of boldfaced games.